INCOME

AN INTRODUCTION TO ECONOMICS

INCOME

An Introduction
to Economics

BY

A. C. PIGOU, M.A.

SOMETIME PROFESSOR OF POLITICAL ECONOMY
IN THE UNIVERSITY OF CAMBRIDGE

GREENWOOD PRESS, PUBLISHERS
WESTPORT, CONNECTICUT

Library of Congress Cataloging in Publication Data

Pigou, Arthur Cecil, 1877-1959.
    Income : an introduction to economics.

    Reprint of the 1966 issue published by Macmillan,
London and St. Martin's Press, New York of a work
first published in 1946.
    Includes bibliographical references.
    1. Income. I. Title.
HB601.P63 1979   339.2   78-21487
ISBN 0-313-20665-1

First edition 1946

Reprinted with the permission of the Macmillan Press
Limited.

Reprinted in 1979 by Greenwood Press, Inc.
51 Riverside Avenue, Westport, CT 06880

Printed in the United States of America

10 9 8 7 6 5 4 3 2 1

PREFATORY NOTE

THIS little book is based on and in the main reproduces seven lectures given in Cambridge at the request of the Professor of Engineering to students in his subject in the Lent Term of 1945. Its purpose is to provide an outline sketch of an important part of economics that shall be intelligible and, if possible, interesting to non-economists. The first chapter, while logically necessary to the development of the argument, is, I am afraid, rather arid; some readers may prefer to start with Chapter II. For the purpose in hand I have thought that no harm, perhaps some good, would be done by retaining the informal style appropriate to what was written to be read aloud. In connection with the few figures cited (*e.g.* on p. 48), the date, set out below, when what follows was prepared for the press, should be borne in mind.

A. C. P.

KING'S COLLEGE, CAMBRIDGE
March 1945

1955. In this reprint some figures more recent than those available in 1945 are given in a note at the end of the book.

CONTENTS

CHAPTER I

THE NATIONAL INCOME: DEFINITION AND MEASUREMENT

MOST of the larger questions in which economists are interested are connected in one way or another with the national income. How big is this? What are the chief influences on which a country's capacity for producing income depends? In what proportions is income made up of or taken out in various sorts of things; and what are the chief influences determining, say, how far it consists in food, clothes, house-room and so on? How is it shared out among the people and on what influences does the way of its sharing-out depend? How is it distributed over time? What part do and should Government authorities play in regard to it? and so on. It is possible, I think, by working along these lines, to give an outline sketch of what economics is chiefly about. That is what in the chapters that follow I shall try to do.

With that programme evidently the first thing needed is to get a clear idea of what we are going to *mean* by income. Perhaps you may think that there is nothing to say about this; that everybody knows perfectly well what income is, that to argue about it is merely splitting hairs. But the thing is not so simple as all that.

Anybody speaking about income in ordinary conversation is likely to have in mind money income: somebody's income is £1000 a year; somebody else's £2000 a year: the income of Great Britain before the war was in the neighbourhood of £4000 millions a year; now it is in the neighbourhood of £8000 millions. But this notion of income as money income does not go very deep. For, after all, people do not value money income for its own sake, but because of the goods and services that it enables them to buy. A man with £1000 a year at one period is as well off in all important senses as a man with £2000 a year in a second period, if in that second period everything costs twice as much as it did in the first. What I said just now about this country's income being in the neighbourhood of £4000 millions a year before the war and of £8000 millions now does not tell us much unless we are able, at least in a rough way, to compare the purchasing power of a pound then and a pound now. In short, what really signifies is not money income, but what money income will buy, or, in the economist's language, not money income but real income.

What, then, is real income? Here is Marshall's broad, general account of it: "The labour and capital of the country acting on its natural resources produces annually a certain net aggregate of commodities, material and immaterial, including services of all kinds. This is the true net national income or revenue of the country, or the national dividend." [1] Note *of the country*, not *of the Government* of the country. Briefly, then, real income in any period consists in the net inflow of goods and services — necessaries and conveniences of life — that accrue during that period.

In this account I have brought in the word *net*. This warns us that, in making an inventory of real income, we must be careful not to reckon in the same thing twice over. Suppose, for instance, that you are interested in the contribution made to the country's real income by the farming industry. You might be inclined to set down for any year the quantities of beef, pork, mutton, milk, wheat, barley, turnips, mangel-wurzels, swedes and so on that farms yielded during that year, and count them all in. But that would be a gross fallacy. Why? Because a lot of the barley, mangel-wurzels and so on were eaten

[1] *Principles of Economics*, 5th edition, p. 524.

2

by the animals, and so embodied in the mutton and pork produced during the year. When you have counted in the pork, you mustn't also count in the stuff that has gone into pigs to make pork. In the same way, when you have counted in the loaves of bread produced during a year, you mustn't also count the wheat that has been produced and been used to make the bread. That is the point of the term *net*. The real income produced by any set of people is, not their gross output per year, or other period, but their gross output *less* such stuff received from other people as is embodied in their gross output.

There is one implication arising out of this which is very important but might be overlooked if one were careless. It is obvious to anybody that the wheat embodied in the bread produced in any year is not something additional to it but is part of it. It is physically embodied in it. But it is possible for things produced by one industry to be embodied in those produced by another in a subtler way than this. Consider the country's output of cloth. Obviously wool is embodied in the cloth in exactly the same way as wheat is embodied in bread. But what of the machinery employed in the textile and clothing trades ? Every year, in the process of spinning wool and weaving cloth, a certain amount of machinery is worn out. This used-up machinery has entered into the fabric of the cloth quite as really as the wool has done. Suppose that a thousand machines are worn out in this way during a year. To avoid double counting you must not reckon as a part of real income all the machines produced during the year, but that number minus the thousand that are worn out. More generally, real income does not include *all* the instruments of production made during the year, but only the excess of those made over the number required to offset wear and tear

Often the substance of what I have been saying is expressed in the statement that net real income consists in gross output minus such part of this as is needed to maintain capital intact. But this is only right if the phrase ' maintain capital intact ' is used in a restricted sense, to mean, not maintaining capital intact absolutely, but maintaining it intact against depletions suffered by it in connection with its use in industry. In reckoning up net real income no deduction must be made to offset damage to capital equipment arising out of entirely outside causes that have nothing to do with the productive use of the equipment ; for example, destruction due to Act of God or the King's enemies. These we treat as capital losses — a separate thing. If we counted them in, we should get absurd results. In the year of an earthquake or war we might have to say that income was negative. That would obviously be a very paradoxical way of speaking.

There is, indeed, a certain awkwardness. Some sorts of productive resources wear away simply by lapse of time, rust and so on, or are exposed to accident, for example, by fire, even when not in use. *These* depletions we do not reckon as capital losses, but as set-offs reducing net income below gross income. The reason is that they are inevitable incidents of holding the equipment for use, whether it is actually in use or not. But there is no rigid line. In England destruction by earthquake would certainly be counted as a capital loss, but, if there was an earthquake on a given scale occurring regularly every three months, the destruction which it did might perhaps be treated as an element in the cost of production, and so be set off against gross income. A good practical rule is that those depletions of capital which business men normally take account of by insuring against them, whether formally or informally, but not others, should be deducted from gross income before net income is reckoned.

There is a connected point, rather important. Food and clothes are essential for the maintenance intact of the labour force. They make good *its* wear and tear. Are we to deduct that from gross income as we do what is needed to keep machines intact ? If we did, net income would work out very small. The answer of practice is, of course, no. This is justified because the wear and tear of human beings, which food is needed to make good, is not, in the main, wear and tear resulting from their being used or held ready for use as productive agents. It is the sort of wear and tear, therefore, that, if it were allowed to take place, should be reckoned as a capital loss having nothing to do with income. This implies that the food and so on which people eat, in spite of the fact that it prevents this loss from occurring, must not be deducted from gross income when we reckon up net income.

There is yet another awkward point. This has to do with equipment growing obsolete on account of more efficient equipment being invented or of machines ceasing to be wanted because the things that they used to make have gone out of fashion. In this case there is no physical wear and tear, such as happens to machinery in use. Physically the equipment is wholly intact, but its value has fallen. The same thing may happen to stocks of goods in dealers' hands — working capital. When bits of capital are physically unchanged but have lost value, are we to say that a part of gross income should be regarded as a set-off against this and deducted before we get net income ? In principle, I am inclined to think, equipment should be regarded as maintained intact so long as it is physically unaltered and that obsolescence should only come in when, on account of it, equipment is thrown out and discarded, this discarding being equivalent to wear and tear. But there are differences of opinion among economists as to what usage is most convenient in this matter. After all, it is only a question of convenience. We can seldom say that one definition is right and another wrong ; only that one is more, another less convenient.

5

Pass on, then, and next notice this. The real income accruing to a group of people in a year consists of two parts : real consumption — the mass of stuff consumed — and real investment — net creations of new capital. Real consumption is necessarily positive ; for negative consumption is inconceivable and nil consumption for any length of time would involve the extinction of mankind. Real investment may be either positive or negative. That is to say, real income may either exceed real consumption, in which case the balance consists of new capital constructs ; or real income may fall short of real consumption. In that case the deficiency is filled by using up existing pieces of capital or by neglecting to maintain capital intact.

This equality, real income equals real consumption plus real investment, is sometimes thought to carry with it an important causal implication ; to imply that any reduction in real consumption brought about by propaganda or Government action necessarily carries with it an equivalent expansion in real investment. This is a gross fallacy. Enforced or induced contraction of consumption *does* necessarily carry with it an equivalent contraction in real income *minus* real investment. But this need not be accomplished through an expansion of real investment. It may be accomplished through a contraction of real income ; or partly in the one way and partly in the other. What will happen in fact depends on the detailed nature of the situation. If we want more investment there is no guarantee that, by conducting an economy campaign, we shall get it. We may get instead less real income ; which implies less employment. This point seems simple enough. But it is not always understood. A failure to understand it on the part of governing persons in this country led to action which made the great slump of 1930–31 more long-drawn-out and more severe than it need have been.

Now for a different problem. Real income, as I have

6

described it, is made up in any period of a stream of goods and services. It is thus evidently not the same thing as the money income of that period. For that is a stream of money receipts. But the two things are related. What is the nature of the relation ? Roughly, we may conceive all the items of real income in any period as sold into the shops by the several producers and then bought out of these shops by their several consumers, who are, of course, the producers of other items. One man sells in a week ten pounds' worth of boots and spends the ten pounds in buying wheat and meat and clothes. This means that the money income is the payment made for, and so the value of, the real income of goods and services. In this way money income *represents* real income ; against every pound of it there stands an equivalent pound's worth of real income.

For an economist this is a natural and convenient use of terms. But, if we are to adopt it, we must add a point to what I have said so far about the definition of real income. I have described this broadly as the net inflow of goods and services becoming available per income period. We need to modify that a little. By convention we do not reckon as real income the whole of this net flow, but only a part of it — only that part of it which is paid for with money or is easily represented in money terms. We exclude the flow of services rendered gratuitously to one another by members of the same family or by friends ; by a man's clothes or furniture to himself ; and so on. If these things were included in real income, money income would be the value, not of the whole of real income, but only of a part of it. Our conventional definition, with certain refinements, particularly one concerning what is called the foreign balance — about which we need not trouble here — allows us to say broadly that aggregate money income is the value or purchase price of aggregate real income. This for the economist is the relation between these two incomes.

But now we come against a point important to statis-
ticians. The economist's money income — what we usually
call social income — which in this way corresponds to real
income, is not identical with money income as understood
by the income tax commissioners. The commissioners
reckon as income and assess to taxation interest received
on war loan securities, gratuitous pensions and so on ;
that is, money incomings not received in exchange for
any contribution of current service and so not represented
by or corresponding to any real income. These incomings
are transfer payments, just as an allowance made by a
father to his son is a transfer payment. If a man with
£1000 a year allows his son £200 a year, the aggregate
income of the two together, both for the economist and
for the income tax commissioners, is not £1200, but £1000.
This is the value of all the real income that there is, namely,
the services rendered by the work and equipment of the
father. But the transfer payments constituted by war
loan interest and gratuitous pensions are not treated by
the income tax commissioners like these other transfer
payments. They are counted as income. The commissioners' money income, therefore, exceeds the money
income — social income — of the economist, to which real
income corresponds, by the amount of these transfer payments. The difference is substantial. According to the
Chancellor of the Exchequer's White Paper for 1943-4,
while national social income was about £8200 millions,
income reckoned inclusive of transfer payments came to
something over £8800 millions — about 7½ per cent more.

There is one other complication. What productive
resources receive for their services is obviously the same
thing looked at the other way round as what people pay for
these services. Therefore, if we ignore time-lags, we may
say that money income as the economist understands it —
social income — is equivalent to and is represented equally

well by the money receipts of productive resources and by the money values of what these resources produce. If there were no taxes or subsidies (which are, of course, negative taxes) paid on commodities there would be no difficulty here. But, where there are commodity taxes, the money value of what productive resources yield may be interpreted in two ways : either as this money value including tax — cum-tax — or as this value ex-tax. Which of these two senses must the term value have in order that the money income of productive resources and the value of their output shall be equivalent ? The answer to this question is not hard to find. A part of the output of productive resources consists of things that are not sold in the market but are made directly for the Government — naval vessels, aircraft and so on. *If we reckon the value of these things at cost*, the rest of the output of productive resources must be valued ex-tax, or, in language now becoming common, at factor cost — not cum-tax. By valuing it cum-tax we should make what is paid for the services of productive resources bigger than what these resources receive for their services ; and this would be self-contradictory.

These points that I have been making about definitions may seem rather academic. In a sense, of course, they are. But they are certainly not unimportant ; because statistics about income and changes of income cannot possibly be worked out satisfactorily unless our definitions are clear-cut. Still, I won't lead you any further along those lines. Turn to a problem of wider sweep. Since money income consists of one thing only, namely money, there can obviously never be any difficulty — given the statistics — about comparing the sizes of money income at different times or at different places where the same money is used. We can always say, in principle, that one money income A is larger than another money income B ; and, further, that one is larger than the other in such-and-such a definite proportion — by 10 or 30 per cent. But, as we saw earlier on, estimates or comparisons of money incomes taken by themselves are not of much use; their significance depends on what purchasing power a unit of money has. Real income, not money income, is what matters. But real income is made up, not of one kind of thing, rather of a great variety of different kinds of things. To compare the sizes of two incomes made up like that is a quite different and much more formidable task than to compare two money incomes. How would you propose to tackle that problem ?

Up to a point the problem is straightforward. If the real income of 1935 contains as much of every single kind of item as the real income of 1930 *and something more besides*, then it is clearly in a strict physical sense the larger of the two. Further, if there is no item of which it contains less than 10 per cent more than the real income of 1930 does, it is again in a strict physical sense at least 10 per cent larger. In the same way, if there is no item in which it falls short of the 1930 real income by more than 10 per cent, it is again in a strict physical sense not more than 10 per cent smaller. Thus, when the facts are known about all the detailed items, we are able to make un-ambiguous physical statements as to limits within which the difference between the sizes of the real incomes of different years lie. In some cases these limits may be very close together, so that, for example, the real income of year 2 is not more than 20 per cent and not less than 15 per cent larger in this physical sense than the real income of year 1. But in other cases the limits may be very wide ; 80 per cent larger, say, on the one side and 50 per cent smaller on the other. With limits as wide as that there is very little to be gained by knowing what they are.

So far we have been unambitious, and the going has at least been safe. But, it is widely thought, we can do better than this by some process of averaging. Here the ground is extremely dangerous and tricky. Since these — as they are called — index number devices are used quite glibly even in newspapers, it may be worth while to look at some of the pitfalls.

In its crudest form the averaging process is worked like this. We choose some base year and represent the quantity of each article entering into the real income of that year by 100. In the next year, if there is half as much of any given article, we represent its quantity by 50; if there is half as much again, by 150; and so on. We then average the figures found for each several article in respect of the second year. If they work out at, say, 130, then — since the average of the base year's figures must obviously be 100 — the real income of the other year is said to be 30 per cent higher. This sounds all right But beware ! Suppose that real income is made up of two sorts of things only, bicycles and hats. The facts are, say, that there are twice as many bicycles in 1935 as in 1930 and half as many hats. We proceed to represent the quantities of each of these things in 1930 by 100. Then the quantity of bicycles in 1935 must be represented by 200 and the quantity of hats by 50. Taking arithmetical averages, we find, then, that real income as a whole, bicycles and hats together, has gone up from $\frac{100 + 100}{2}$ to $\frac{200 + 50}{2}$, that is, by 25 per cent This is a queer consequence to follow from doubling one part of a country's real income plus halving the rest ! But that is not the end of the queerness. Let us use 100 to represent the quantities of bicycles and hats in 1935 instead of in 1930. Then in 1930 the quantity of bicycles must be represented by 50 and the quantity of hats by 200. On that showing the arithmetical average of the two is 125 in 1930 and 100 in 1935, that is, the real income of 1930 is 25 per cent larger than that of 1935, instead of the real income of 1935 being 25 per cent larger than that of 1930! And it is purely arbitrary choice whether we use 1930 or 1935 as our base year, the year for which the quantities are to be represented by 100. Evidently there is something wrong. This does not make sense. What is wrong?

Let us go back a bit. Suppose, to take a specially simple case, that the actual numbers of bicycles and of hats in 1930 are equal, say ten of each, and that in 1935 there are five bicycles and twenty hats. When we take 1930 as our base year and represent the quantities of both bicycles and hats then by 100, what we are in effect doing is treating one bicycle as equivalent to — as equally important with — one hat. On that basis the real income of 1930 is equivalent to twenty hats and in 1935 to twenty-five hats; 25 per cent larger in 1935 than in 1930. But, when we take 1935 as base year and represent the quantities of both bicycles and hats then by 100, we are in effect treating one bicycle as equivalent to four hats, so that in 1930 real income is equivalent to fifty hats and in 1935 to forty hats; 25 per cent larger in 1930 than in 1935.

Do you see what all this shows? It shows that, on this index number method of approach, the question how much bigger or smaller the real income of bicycles and hats together is in 1935 than in 1930 is ambiguous; has in fact no meaning until we specify how many hats are to be considered, for the purposes of our calculation, equivalent to one bicycle. So soon as we specify that, the question is unambiguous and has a perfectly clear-cut answer. But, of course, the question is a different one, and so also naturally is the answer, for each several number of hats that we choose to regard as equivalent to one bicycle.

This whole method then collapses unless we are able to find some satisfactory principle on which to decide how many hats shall be taken as equivalent to one bicycle.

Can we find such a principle? Obviously no physical test is available. Comparisons by weight or volume would be ridiculous. What, then, are we to look for? The natural *prima facie* answer is that we should somehow make use of comparative values. A common plan, in constructing this kind of index number, is to weight the quantities of the several items by their aggregate values, that is, by the amounts of expenditure on them. If the numbers of bicycles and of hats in the year upon which we are operating are equal, this implies that we are treating one bicycle as equivalent to that number of hats which the price of one bicycle will buy. If the numbers are not equal, this method of weighting implies treating one bicycle as equivalent to the number of hats that the price of a bicycle will buy, multiplied by the total number of bicycles, divided by the total number of hats. Will this sort of thing serve? There are serious difficulties of principle. Would it not, for example, be more reasonable to measure the comparative importance of, say, bread and wine to a country by what its citizens would be willing to pay for them rather than go without them altogether than by what they actually do pay? And ought not some account of the fact that some things are bought chiefly by rich, others chiefly by poor people? I cannot discuss these matters here. But there is another difficulty that lies on the surface. As a rule, if the comparative quantities of bicycles and hats in two years are different, the comparative expenditures upon them will be different also. If, then, we agree to settle how many bicycles are equivalent to one hat by reference to these comparative expenditures, which year's expenditures are we to use? For a comparison of the real income, say of 1930 and 1935, the relative expenditures in 1930 have no better and no worse claim to serve as a test of importance than the relative expenditures of 1935. No doubt, if we like, we can use some sort of average to bring into account the relative expenditures of both years. But whatever we do in this way — particularly since there are several different rival sorts of average — would be arbitrary, not grounded on any principle. We are thus faced with a number of alternative figures for comparing the sizes or real income in 1930 and 1935, and there is no clear reason for preferring any one of them to any other.

With all these complications, I think you will agree, the method of comparing the sizes of different real incomes which I have been describing and discussing — a method on which most index numbers in actual use directly or indirectly depend — has extremely shaky foundations. I don't think it has been a waste of time to show this. It is quite useful to realise that what writers in newspapers think they know all about and what at first sight seems perfectly easy and straightforward is sometimes in fact obscure.

The practical upshot is plain. Once we abandon the sure ground of physical fact we are likely to find ourselves juggling with symbols in an extremely foggy atmosphere. So long as we stand on that ground, we are entitled to say what I said earlier on. I will repeat it. If the real income of 1935 contains as much of every single kind of item as the real income of 1930 *and something more besides*, then it is the larger of the two. Further, if there is no item of which it contains less than 10 per cent more than the real income of 1930 does, it is at least 10 per cent larger. In the same way, if there is no item in which it falls short of the 1930 real income by more than 10 per cent, it is not more than 10 per cent smaller. Thus, when the facts are known about all the detailed items, we are able to make unambiguous physical statements as to the limits within which the difference between the sizes of the real incomes of different years lie. If we try to go beyond that we get into serious, I don't say insurmountable, troubles, but troubles which can only be got over by using special definitions and conventions that contain arbitrary elements — certainly not a fit subject for lectures intended to be elementary.

Now, you may remember that among the subjects I proposed for discussion one was : What are the chief influences upon which the country's capacity to produce real income depends ? If there is all this difficulty about comparing the sizes of different real incomes, must there not be at least as great difficulty about tackling that problem ? Fortunately no. Between two years some technical development, say, takes place. As a consequence, the quantities of the various items contained in real income stand in different proportions to one another in the second year from what they did in the first. It may be that there is a larger quantity of some items in the second and a smaller quantity of others. In that case we cannot say, speaking in physical terms, either that real income as a whole is larger in the second year than in the first or that it is smaller. But this does not mean that we cannot say whether the technical development has improved or worsened the country's capacity to produce real income. Thus, suppose that the 1930 real income consisted of a hundred bicycles and a hundred hats. In 1935 a technical change is introduced which makes it much easier to produce bicycles. People may be so keen on having bicycles, which are now cheaper, that productive power has to be switched from hat-making to bicycle-making ; so that the new real income is, say, 250 bicycles and 80 hats. Since there are fewer hats than before, we can't say, speaking physically, that the second real income is bigger than the first. But we can say that the technical change has rendered our productive resources capable of producing more real income of the pattern of 1930, with equal numbers of hats and bicycles, and also capable of producing more on the pattern of 1935 with bicycles and hats in the proportion of 25 to 8. That is to say, it has rendered us capable of producing more real income of *either* of these patterns ; and, it is easy to see further, not less real income of any pattern. It is, therefore, quite proper to say that we have become capable of producing more real income without qualification. Inability to distinguish which of two actual real incomes is physically the larger does not imply inability to recognise influences that increase the income-producing power of a country's resources. We cannot, indeed, as a rule say that a particular development of technique has made that power larger than before by some definite percentage ; because, among other things, it will, almost certainly, have increased our power to produce real incomes of different patterns in different degrees. But we can say that it has increased our power to produce real income in *some* degree or by *some* percentage. That is enough for my purpose. Provided we are able to do that, the way is clear for my next chapter. There I shall no longer be dealing with definitions and logical implications, but with straightforward industrial facts.

CHAPTER II

INTERNAL INFLUENCES AFFECTING INCOME-
GETTING POWER

IN this chapter I shall give a general account of the chief influences on which the capacity of any country to produce a larger or smaller real income depends. I shall speak as though we had to do with a closed economy isolated from the rest of the world ; postponing to the next chapter the effects of foreign trade. As a first step we want some sort of picture of what a country's productive resources are.

Among these the most obvious is the physical environment, provided by nature, in which the people live. This embraces a great number of elements. There is the surface of the land, with its income of rain and sunshine, its power of producing vegetable, and sustaining animal life ; sometimes a fertile valley, sometimes a hillside, sometimes a waterless plain. There are the rivers and seas and lakes, from which fish can be taken and across which boats can move ; and waterfalls, or, more strictly, configurations of the land adapted to waterfalls, which may yield power. All this large group of natural resources the classical economists were accustomed to hold together under a single name, the fundamental factor of production, Land.

Secondly, alongside of productive resources provided by nature, there is another very important group, the instruments of production and stocks of consumption goods built up on the basis of nature's raw material by man's efforts. Under this head fall all such things as roads, canals, railway lines, telegraph and telephone equipment, factory buildings, houses, waterworks, gas plants, machinery of every kind, half-made goods in process through furnaces and mills, stores of finished articles in warehouses and shops, agricultural tools and so on. This collection of miscellaneous things economists have grouped together as a second great factor of production, Capital, or, more strictly, material capital The logical thing to do would be to reckon in here everything made by man that is held as a stock of wealth. But, in order to fit in with common usage, economists do not usually take so wide a sweep as that. Thus Marshall proposes " to count as part of Capital from the social point of view all things other than land which yield income that is usually reckoned as such in common discourse ; together with similar things in public ownership, such as Government factories ; the term Land being taken to include all free gifts of nature, such as mines, fisheries, etc., which yield income. Thus it [capital] includes all things held for trade purposes, whether machinery, raw material or finished goods ; theatres and hotels ; home farms and houses ; but not furniture or clothes owned by those who use them. For the former are and the latter are not commonly regarded as yielding income by the world at large, as is shown by the practice of the income tax commissioners." [1] I recommend to you that definition. But, whether you like it or dislike it, in the light of it you will probably agree that capital is *not*, as it was once elegantly defined, " money taken from the labouring classes, which, being given to army tailors and such-like, enables them to keep foxhounds and to trace their descent to the Normans ".[2]

Thirdly, there are to be distinguished the productive powers of human beings themselves : their hand power and their brain power ; their capacity to perform various sorts of muscular work or to direct it in various ways, to make plans, to design instruments, to organise, to arrange,

[1] *Principles of Economics*, 5th edition, p. 78.
[2] By Cobbett. Cf. Leslie Stephen, *The English Utilitarians*, vol. ii, p. 131.

to control. All this, in the widest and most inclusive sense, we group as a third great factor of production, Labour, or, more strictly, labour power.

These three great groups, land, capital and labour, constitute the fundamental triad of the classical economists. But there is besides what can conveniently be brought under these heads a fourth very important group. Men live, not merely in a material environment, but also in an environment of ideas. Their productive power depends in great part upon this environment ; their knowledge of natural law and mechanical technique ; the various schemes of organisation by which they are held together in a co-operative network. It is possible, no doubt, with a little straining, to bring these things under the head of material capital and labour power, but some people prefer to put them in an extra group, that might perhaps be headed immaterial capital. Whether or not we should do this is a secondary matter. The essential thing is that among productive resources a great, indeed a dominant, place is occupied by the current stock of ideas. I shall return to this at the end of the chapter.

These several agents or factors of production that I have been describing are most conveniently thought of as an enduring stock, out of whose joint working there is generated every year that flow of services and goods of which real income consists. In perfectly steady conditions the stock of productive agents would always remain the same, each generation of men, as they die, being replaced by the next, and all machines, as they become worn out, being in the same way replaced by new ones. In actual conditions the stock, of course, undergoes change. Apart from periods of war, we are accustomed to the volume of capital equipment, as well as the volume of labour power, expanding from decade to decade. But in any event, whether it is stationary or changing, the stock of productive resources constitute, so to speak, the generating plant by whose agency the annual flow of real income is brought into being.

If we look at the matter in this way, we see at once that, among influences on which a country's capacity to produce a larger or smaller real income depends, a dominant one is the amount of the several sorts of productive resources that it possesses. The more and better its land, the more and better its capital equipment, and the more numerous and more efficient its population of working age, say from 15 to 65, the larger will be the annual flow of real income in the aggregate that it is capable of producing. I put in the words ' in the aggregate ' to remind you that not all influences which make real income in the aggregate larger necessarily make real income per head larger. Large possessions of land or capital do, indeed, promote large real income in both senses. But enlargement in the population of working age unaccompanied by increased individual efficiency, while it is fairly sure to make aggregate income larger, is likely, unless at the same time there is a corresponding enlargement in the stock of equipment, to make income per head smaller But that is by the way. The essential — and obvious — thing is that, the larger is the volume of any sort of productive resource, the larger will be the amount of real income that it can produce. It follows that all influences which make these resources larger are also influences indirectly increasing our income-getting power. It would be easy to say a good deal about what these influences are, and particularly about those that affect the scale of capital and the efficiency of the population of working age. Obviously public policy as regards investment, on the one hand in material capital, on the other in the training and education of people's minds and bodies, may play a large part here. But I can't discuss these things now, and shall pass at once to something different and perhaps less obvious.

It is not only on the volume of its several sorts of resources that a country's capacity to produce real income depends. That depends also on the forms into which the fundamental factors of labour power and capital are organised, especially on the manner and degree in which they are specialised to a narrow range of jobs. Since people want, not a single thing only, but a great number of different things, the aggregate of productive resources belonging to all of them together must, of course, be spread over a multitude of different things. But that tells us nothing about what individual units of productive resources, individual work-people, for example, will do. Suppose that work in the aggregate is to be distributed in the proportions of X to food-making, Y to machine-making, Z to transport service, and so on. This is compatible *either* with every workman spreading his time over these different sorts of work in the proportions X, Y, Z and so on, *or* with X men being engaged exclusively on the first, Y men exclusively on the second and Z men exclusively on the third. But it makes an enormous difference to aggregate output which of these two types of arrangement is adopted. In general, the specialised arrangement is much more productive than the all-round arrangement and enables a much bigger real income to be yielded by a given volume of productive resources. Everybody knows that this is so. I want to ask why it is so, what are the circumstances that make specialisation technically productive. Two main reasons may be distinguished.

First, people — and the same thing is true of pieces of land — are not all alike in inborn endowments. I don't merely mean that some men are better at everything than other men. The inborn *relative* capacities of different men — and different pieces of land — for various kinds of activity are different. One man is physically stronger but mentally feebler than another; one man's brain is relatively much better adapted to mathematical work as compared with classical work than another's ; just as one piece of land is relatively much better suited for wheat-growing as against pasture than another piece. These differences in relative capacities may still exist even though one man or one piece of land is absolutely better than a second at *everything*. Einstein may be better at football as well as at physics than Mr. Jones, but his superiority at physics is probably much greater than his superiority at football. It is easy to see that, whenever man A is relatively better at making hats and man B relatively better at making bicycles, there will be more hats and more bicycles if, instead of both men dividing their time equally between hats and bicycles, A spends most of his time on hats and B most of his on bicycles. Extending the argument, it is easy to see further that, when there are a large number of men, the biggest output all round will be produced if most people concentrate all their time on those things at which relatively to other people they are best endowed. In spite of Einstein's being better than Jones at both physics and football, a benevolent dictator would not only keep Jones off physics but also Einstein off football. As Mr. Henry Ford once put it : " The minute subdivision of industry permits a strong man or a skilled man always to use his strength or skill. In the old hand industry a skilled man spent a good part of his time at unskilled work. That was a waste." [1]

Secondly, even if there were no inborn differences in the relative capacities of different men for doing different things, their separation into groups specialised to different things would, nevertheless, greatly benefit output all round. The most obvious reason for this is that training and practice at anything greatly increases a man's capacity for it ; so that, if you have ten men all with exactly similar natural endowments, you will get much more out

[1] *My Life and Work*, p. 208.

of them if you persuade each of them to spend all his time on one thing than if each of them spends one-tenth of his time at each thing. This is pretty obvious. If you find a man writing articles in newspapers about strategy on Monday, birth control on Tuesday, astronomy on Wednesday and so on throughout the week, you may be fairly sure that all the articles are worthless. In the prospectus of an institution which shall be nameless I found recently a gentleman, of whom I had not previously heard, proposing to give instruction in the following subjects : French, Geography, English, Civics, History, Literature, Physics, Economics. I did not feel tempted to become a student in that institution. No ; specialisation is good for production because practice promotes skill. I am bound to quote here Adam Smith's famous illustration. "The division of labour," he writes — division of labour is, of course, specialisation looked at in reverse — "the division of labour, by reducing everyman's business to some one simple operation, and by making this operation the sole employment of his life, necessarily increases very much the dexterity of the workman. A common smith, who, though accustomed to handle the hammer, has never been used to make nails, if upon some particular occasion he is obliged to attempt it, will scarce, I am assured, be able to make above two or three hundred nails in a day, and those very bad ones. A smith who has been accustomed to make nails, but whose sole or principal business has not been that of a nailer, can seldom with his utmost diligence make more than 800 or 1000 nails in a day. I have seen several boys under 20 years of age who had never exercised any other trade but that of making nails, and who, when they exerted themselves, could make, each of them, upwards of 2300 nails in a day." [1]

A word of qualification should perhaps be added here. Like other good things it is possible for specialisation to

[1] *Wealth of Nations* (Scott's edition), vol i, p. 9.

be pressed too far — so far as to damage, not benefit, efficiency. A mountaineer who is only a rock expert and useless on ice, or vice versa, will be a great handicap to an Alpine party. In some kinds of intellectual work, too, specialisation may be carried too far. A surgeon who knows everything about one's liver and nothing at all about anything else may want to extract one's liver when it is really a kidney that is misbehaving. Again, in some fields of work it is general ability rather than specialised ability that is important. Thus politicians rarely specialise. The same man is equally competent to control, one after the other, the Board of Trade, the War Office, the Board of Education, the Exchequer, India, the Admiralty ! But politicians, of course, are exceptional men. For ordinary men, up to a high point, specialisation usually makes them more efficient.

But it is not only among men, the agent of production Labour, that specialisation acts strongly to promote income-getting power. The same thing is true of the agent of production Capital in the form of machinery and tools. Specialisation, division of labour, means splitting up industrial operations into a large number of small separate parts, each carried out by machines specially adapted to it, working on it continuously, and not adapted to anything else. This is extremely important. As one writer puts it : " The main object of the division of labour is no longer so much to develop the dexterity of the human operator as to enable the continuous employment of the highly specialised machine. Industrial progress consists, therefore, at the present day, largely in the continuous advance towards a greater and greater measure of what is known as *standardisation* ".[1] A very good example of this is given by Mr. Henry Ford in his autobiography. He is describing the process of painting the rear axle of the old T model Ford car. A plan that on the face of

[1] D. H. Robertson, *Control of Industry*, p. 18.

things would seem fairly effective is that sometimes adopted for agricultural implements, simply dipping them, when ready, into a large tank full of paint. But that was not good enough for Mr. Ford. This is what he writes : " Painting the rear axle once gave some trouble. It used to be dipped by hand into a tank of enamel. This required several handlings and the service of two men. Now one man . . . merely hangs the assembly on a moving chain, which carries it up over the enamel tank, two levers then thrust thimbles over the ends of the ladle shaft, the paint tank rises six feet, immerses the axle, returns to position, and the axle goes on to the drying oven. The whole cycle of operations now takes just thirteen seconds." [1] I hink you would be interested to read that book, *Henry Ford, My Life and Work*.

Granted, then, that specialisation of work-people and machines each to a small range of jobs, to which they are or can become closely adapted, is an important means of increasing productive power, what conditions are best suited to bring this specialisation about ? Sometimes it is, if one may so speak, an original gift of nature. Among ants the various classes, the soldiers, the workers and so on, are specialised to particular ranges of work by their physiological structure ; and, though there are not among human beings demarcations so sharp as this, there are some demarcations. No man, for example, however keenly he may desire it, can ever successfully become a mother. Further, it is not difficult to imagine societies in which individual specialisations are arranged for and decreed by a governing authority. Mr. H. G. Wells's *The First Men in the Moon* gives an excellent picture of this kind of thing. Children at birth are collected and subjected, some to one, some to another system of dieting and training to turn them into soldiers, mathematicians, coal-miners and so on in whatever proportions the Govern-

[1] *Loc. cit.*, p. 89.

C

ment considers appropriate. But leave these things aside. In the modern world specialisation — division of labour — in the main exists because people, apart altogether from Government decrees, choose that it shall exist. What conditions are required to make them choose so ?

First and foremost is the disposition peculiar to mankind to truck, barter or exchange. If it were not for this disposition, since nobody could get anything he wanted except by making it for himself, everybody would have to make for himself everything that he wanted. He would *have* to be an all-round man ; it would be impossible for him to be a specialist. I come back again to Adam Smith : " Without the disposition to truck, barter and exchange every man must have procured to himself every necessary and conveniency of life which he wanted. All must have had the same duties to perform and the same work to do, and there could have been no such difference of employment as could alone give occasion to any great difference of talents. . . . Many tribes of animals, acknowledged to be all of the same species, derive from nature a much more remarkable distinction of genius than what, antecedent to custom and education, appears to take place among men. By nature a philosopher is not in genius and disposition half so different from a street porter as a mastiff is from a greyhound, or a greyhound from a spaniel, or this last from a shepherd's dog. Those different tribes of animals, however, though all of the same species, are scarce any use to one another. . . . The effects of their different geniuses and talents, for want of the power or disposition to barter and exchange, cannot be brought into a common stock and do not in the least contribute to the better accommodation and conveniency of the species." [1]

But this is not all. Though the disposition to truck, barter and exchange is a *necessary* condition for any

[1] *Wealth of Nations* (Scott's edition), vol. i, p. 17.

degree of specialisation to be developed, it is not a *sufficient* condition. There are also needed arrangements that allow exchanges to be made. If people were completely isolated, each on a separate island, however much they wanted to specialise and exchange their specialities, they would not be able to do so. Each of them would *have* to make shift at doing for himself all the various sorts of jobs that he wanted done. Generalising from this, we see at once that the extent to which specialisation and division of labour, whether of men or of machines, can and will be carried, depends, not only on people's readiness to exchange if they can, but also on the facilities that exist for conducting exchanges.

Thus it depends in the first instance on the size of the market. Here is Adam Smith again : " When the market is very small, no person can have any encouragement to dedicate himself entirely to one employment, for want of the power to exchange all that surplus part of the produce of his own labour, which is over and above his own consumption, for such parts of the produce of other men's labour as he has occasion for. . . . In the lone houses and very small villages, which are scattered about in so desert a country as the Highlands of Scotland, every farmer must be butcher, baker and brewer for his own family. In such situations we can scarce expect to find even a smith, a carpenter or a mason within less than twenty miles of another of the same trade. The scattered families that live at eight or ten miles distance from the nearest of them must learn to perform themselves a great number of little pieces of work, for which, in more populous countries, they would call in the assistance of those workmen." [1] In the same way, unless a very large number of motor cars were being made — unless there was a large market for them — it would not pay anybody to set up, and nobody would set up, a highly elaborated

[1] *Ibid.*, p. 18.

mass-production organisation with specialised machines for making every small part of one type of car, on the pattern of Ford or Morris.

But we have not done yet. The size of the market is not a thing in itself, which just is what it is, with nothing more to be said about it. It depends on something else. With a given population spread over a given space, it depends on how good the means of communication are. Until you can send things about fairly cheaply and quickly, they *must* be made in the neighbourhood where they are going to be used. With bad communications, therefore, unless there are a great number of people living close together, you can't have any high degree of specialisation. But with bad communications you can't have a great number of people living close together, because it would be impossible for them to get the food they need. Therefore a necessary condition of any high degree of specialisation, or division of labour, is good means of communication. This, of course, includes not merely trains and ships, but all the devices that are always being developed for enabling perishable goods to be carried about the world without going bad — bottling processes, canning processes, cooling processes, freezing processes and all the rest.

But even that is not all. You need, besides good communication, an organised machinery of exchange. This includes laws that will check breaches of contract; because people often want to exchange something now against the promise of something later on. Unless that promise is somehow safeguarded, they won't make that sort of exchange except with personal friends. Further, laws of this kind are of no use unless they are enforceable. So you also have to have a system of law courts to adjudicate on disputes and a police force to secure that the decisions of the courts are enforced.

Yet again, it is important that there should be some

generally acceptable medium of exchange. This enables trade to be conducted without the man who wants to sell so many hats having to meet a man who wants to buy exactly that number of hats — and to buy them too by selling exactly that collection of things which the seller of the hats wants to buy ; without the need, in technical language, for a double coincidence between the wants and offers of the several exchangers.

The great importance of this is easily seen if we picture to ourselves the difficulties of direct barter. These are excellently displayed in a passage from an American book about money. The inconveniences of barter — the direct exchange of goods for goods — are illustrated in Lieutenant Cameron's account of his difficulties in buying a boat in Africa : " Syde's agent wished to be paid in ivory, of which I had none ; but I found that Mohammed Ibn Salib had ivory and wanted cloth. Still, as I had no cloth, this did not assist me greatly until I heard that Mohammed Ibn Gharib had cloth and wanted wire. This I fortunately possessed. So I gave Ibn Gharib the requisite amount of wire ; whereupon he handed over cloth to Ibn Salib, who in his turn gave Syde's agent the wished-for ivory. Then he allowed me to have the boat." This case exemplifies the main inconvenience of barter, namely, that of finding a man who not only wants what you have to sell, but has for sale what you want to buy. " Textbooks on money ", the writers go on, " have usually pictured the difficulties of the imaginary hatter, in the imaginary days before there was any medium of exchange, who wanted to buy a house, but who sought in vain for anybody who wanted as many hats as the house was worth. To-day the difficulty of carrying on internal trade without a medium of exchange would be even greater, because most of those who wish to buy goods have no goods whatever to offer as payment. In the shoe factory, for example, there is a bookkeeper, and a sales manager, and a cutter, and a finisher, and a night watchman ; and no one of them produces anything that he can offer to the butcher in exchange for a chop. The butcher does not want their products or their services, any more than he wants the poet's masterpiece. Much less does he desire the admirable statement which the accountant has drawn up for the furrier across the way. Neither does the accountant want his pay in furs, nor the jeweller's office-boy his wages in wedding rings. The only way to satisfy everybody is by means of an interposed something which everybody knows that everybody else will accept in exchange for whatever goods and services they have to sell."[1]

All this that I have been saying has been centred on the idea of specialisation — the division of labour. This, I have argued, is a dominant factor in determining the scale of real income that our productive resources are able to produce. What other factors are there ? This is one. We will be able to produce more, the more nearly firms engaged in our various industries approach what has been called optimum size. Optimum size is that size at which average cost of production is a minimum. Of course, this size is not the same for all sorts of firms, not the same, for example, in steel-making as in cotton-spinning. There are different optimum sizes in different conditions, just as among animals there is one optimum size for an elephant and another for a bumble-bee. An elephant the size of a bumble-bee would be extremely inefficient. So, by reason of the structure of its breathing apparatus, would a bumble-bee the size of an elephant. What the optimum size for a firm in any particular case is varies according to what the firm is making, what the state of industrial technique is, what degree of managerial skill is available, what types of organisation are available — private firm or joint-stock company — and so on. But

[1] Foster and Catchings, *The Circuit Flow of Money*, pp. 35-7.

in any given set of conditions there is *some* one — possibly more than one — size of firm which is optimum in the sense that it makes average cost of production a minimum That being so, it is plain that, so far as firms are of a different size from the optimum in this sense, some productive resources are being wasted. By rearranging the sizes of firms we could get the same output with a smaller use of resources ; and so some of them would be set free for making something else

Now what determines the relation of the actual size of firms to optimum size ? If competition were perfectly effective, any firm that was either too big or too small would be under-sold in the market by rivals. In this way a pressure would be set up tending to make the generality of firms approach closely towards optimum size ; just as elephants and bumble-bees of any given species do. But, so far as competition is not perfectly effective, considerable departures from optimum size are likely to be found. With some sorts of imperfect competition firms will tend to be too small individually and too numerous. It may be that this is true of retail shops. More obviously, when there is a chance of setting up a powerful monopoly and exacting high prices from the public, a firm — or a concern — may become too big, in the sense that, if it were smaller, its average cost would be lower. This happens because the concern can gain more by being big enough to exercise monopoly power than it loses by being too big to achieve minimum average cost. If the exercise of monopoly power to push up prices could be prevented by State action, this influence making for unsuitable size would be abolished, and, so far, we might expect the nation's productive resources to yield a larger output.

Turn to another thing. At any time in any given state of technical knowledge there will be some methods of production — ways of combining capital and labour and so on — that are more effective than any others, so that, when they are adopted, there is a bigger output per unit of productive resources than could be got otherwise. If competition were perfectly effective, it would exert a strong pressure to get these best methods adopted everywhere. Firms that did not adopt them would be under-sold in the market, and so squeezed out by those that did. But in actual life there is a good deal of frictional resistance to change, and competition is not perfectly effective. Consequently, in many places inferior methods of production go on being used, though better methods are known and are in use elsewhere. This is specially likely to happen in such an industry as agriculture, where the different producers are widely scattered and, for some products, serve rather narrow markets. That is why the State sometimes makes an organised effort to spread a knowledge of the best methods by exhibitions, photographs, demonstration trains, lectures, special arrangements for providing farmers with selected types of seed, and so on. The more nearly, by these or other devices, average practice in any industry can be brought up to the level of the best known practice, the larger the output of our productive resources will be.

This leads on naturally to my last point. Our resources will be able to produce more real income, not merely as the best of the known techniques of production come to be more widely used, but also as still better techniques are discovered. This means the advance of scientific knowledge ; not merely secondary scientific knowledge, the *application* of fundamental principles — technical improvements, inventions and so on — but primary scientific knowledge about the principles themselves ; that pure science, which lies behind applied science, and out of which in the last resort applied science springs. So we come back at the end to what I spoke of much earlier in this chapter, the immaterial capital of ideas. Here is the central thought in Marshall's words : " Ideas, whether those of art and science or those embodied in practical appliances, are the most ' real ' of the gifts that each generation receives from its predecessor. The world's material wealth would quickly be replaced if it were destroyed but the ideas by which it was made were retained. If, however, the ideas were lost but not the material wealth, then that would dwindle and the world would go back to poverty. And most of our knowledge of mere facts could quickly be recovered if it were lost but the constructive ideas of thought remained ; while, if the ideas perished, the world would enter again on the dark ages." [1]

Since this chapter has covered a good deal of ground it may be well to summarise the main points. I have been trying to disentangle the chief elements, other than those connected with foreign dealings, on which a country's income-getting power depends. First and most obvious are the amount and quality of the productive resources, Labour in the widest sense, Capital and Land, that the country possesses. Secondly, given these resources, income-getting power is enormously enhanced by the development of division of labour, that is to say specialisation to limited tasks of individual units of them. This is made possible by the fact that human beings, as distinct from other animals, have a propensity to truck, barter or exchange. It is helped by whatever enables this propensity to be exercised ; especially the development of cheap and rapid means of communication ; well drawn and properly enforced legal rules about property and contract ; and the establishment of a generally accepted current money. Income-getting power will also be larger the more closely the size of individual firms in the various industries approaches to what is for those industries the most effective size ; and the more widely improved techniques and methods of organisation

[1] *Principles of Economics*, 5th edition, p. 780.

developed by the best of them come to be known about and practised by the others. Behind all these things and dominant over them, the factor on which income-getting power like much else ultimately depends, is knowledge, thought, ideas. In the beginning was and in the end is, ὁ λόγος, the Word.

CHAPTER III

EXTERNAL INFLUENCES AFFECTING INCOME-
GETTING POWER

FOR an isolated country real income would be simply the
net annual output of that country's productive resources.
But for a country connected with an outside world that
is not so. Part of its real income consists of goods imported
in exchange for current exports of home-made goods and
services ; and another part consists, or may consist, of
goods due to us as interest on investments made abroad
in earlier years. These international dealings have an
obvious bearing on its income-getting power. It is from
this angle, not with regard to their bearing on the proportion in which this power is from time to time exercised
— that is a quite different problem — that I want to
approach them here. But, before that, there are some
preliminary matters of a general kind that have to be
discussed.

First as to the machinery through which these dealings
are worked. If everybody who brought in imports paid
for them individually by exports of British goods or
receipts for interest on foreign investments there would
be no difficulty. But in actual life people engaged in
foreign dealings don't directly barter parcels of imports
against parcels of exports. One man sends coal or manufactured goods to a foreign customer ; a different man
purchases wheat in Canada and has it shipped to England.
There is usually no direct connection between the two
men. How then do exports come to provide means of
payment for imports ?

The broad answer is quite simple. What happens in
effect is that English exporters obtain against their exports

claims on so many dollars, francs and so on, and then sell these claims for English money to those Englishmen who want to pay for goods they have bought abroad for importation here. Thus English exporters are ultimately paid in English money and foreign exporters in foreign money ; which is what they both want. If the claims on dollars, francs and so on, that English exporters earn by their exports, are exactly equivalent to what English importers need for buying their imports, there is no gap to fill up on either side. Otherwise, of course, there is a gap. But, in any case, the whole of the imports, if imports have less value than exports, and the whole of the exports, if exports have less value than imports, are financed out of the proceeds of the sale of whichever of the two — imports or exports — have the greater value. Of course, there are a number of technical details connected with these arrangements which are important for practice ; and, of course, the processes which I have described may be obstructed by various sorts of exchange control. But what I have said gives the essence of the thing. Exports and imports are exchanged against one another up to the point at which all the imports or all the exports have been used up.

The next thing to get clear about is this. In connection with international dealings we frequently come across the phrase ' the balance of trade '. What does this mean ? In what sense, if any, is there a balance ? Consider first the trade relations between one particular country and another particular country. Between these it is easy to see there need not be a balance in any sense. Even if there is no borrowing or lending, there is nothing to prevent a large and permanent excess of imports to A from B over exports to B from A from being established. For this excess may be offset by an equivalent deficiency of imports to A from C below exports to C from A. Here is a passage illustrating this from one of the World

36

surveys of the League of Nations Secretariat written some ten years ago (1934–5) : " Denmark's imports of fodder from cereal-producing countries and of industrial products from Germany are being paid for by exports of bacon and dairy products to the United Kingdom. Germany has a large trade deficit with overseas countries on account of the primary products she requires, but depends upon the European market for her exports of manufactured articles. Belgium and Czechoslovakia are net importers of raw materials from overseas countries and of industrial products from Germany, but net exporters to several other European countries. Poland is also a net importer of various raw materials from India, Australia and the Argentine, but a net exporter of foodstuffs, timber and coal to various European countries, particularly the United Kingdom and Scandinavia. Egypt acquires an export surplus in her trade with the United Kingdom, France and a few other great consumers of the long-staple Egyptian cotton, and employs this surplus in purchases from other countries which are best suited to meet her special requirements. India has to make large debt payments in the United Kingdom ; but the export surplus required for these payments is not obtained in trade with that country (India has in fact an import surplus with the United Kingdom), but with other consumers of Indian products in all continents. The United States have normally a large surplus of exports to Europe, which is only partly offset by her payments to Europe on account of tourists' expenditure and emigrants' remittances : before 1929, a large share of this export surplus was employed in financing the United States imports of raw materials from, and loans to, other continents. . . ." In *The Network of World Trade*, published for the League of Nations in 1943, it is said that normally 70 per cent of all trade in merchandise was bi-lateral ; triangular or multilateral trade represented about 25 per cent during the 1920's. Further,

" much bi-lateral trade in manufactured goods is dependent for its existence upon the multi-lateral trade, by which the necessary raw materials are acquired ".[1]

But this is really by the way. What about the trade of a single country, say Great Britain, with the rest of the world taken as a whole ? It is customary to distinguish between income account, which is concerned with current inward and outward obligations, and capital account, which records changes in capital or capital indebtedness. When income account and capital account are taken together, England's account with the rest of the world *must* balance ; for the simple reason that any obligation which is not met becomes *ipso facto* a capital debt. But it is not in the least necessary for England's, or any other country's, income account with the rest of the world to balance. England may be lending abroad or it may be borrowing abroad. In the first case, the value of its exports of goods and services plus its claims to interest from foreigners will exceed the value of its imports; in the second case, will fall short of this. Down to the 1914–18 war and again afterwards until the great slump England's income account with the rest of the world was in nearly all years in credit. That is, we were using a part of the proceeds of our exports and of our claims to interest, not to bring in imports, but to add to our foreign investments. In the quinquennium ending with 1930 these additions ran to something like £100 millions a year. But since 1931 England did not add to her foreign investments. On the contrary, in order to meet her current purchases, she had to deplete these investments in most years to a slight extent.

We can now get on to our main business. What is the fundamental significance of international dealings for national income-getting power ? Imagine a country with given productive resources ; and contrast what its situa-

[1] *Loc cit.*, p. 88.

tion would be if it had no outside contacts at all with what it is when foreign dealings are open to it. The difference is that it is now able to get a number of things by the indirect process of making something else and selling it abroad, instead of having to make everything that its people want directly for itself. Conditions might be such that there would be no significance in this. It might cost exactly the same effort to get things by the indirect process as by the direct one. In that case, though the channels of international trade were open, there would be no point in using them, and in fact they would not be used. This would be so if, with no trade at all taking place, the comparative values of all sorts of things measured in the local moneys of the different countries were exactly the same ; bicycles, for example, exactly twice as valuable as hats everywhere. But it is very unlikely that, with no trade taking place, the comparative values of all sorts of things would in fact be the same everywhere. For one thing, natural resources may exist in one country, but not in another, that are specially favourable to the production of certain commodities. If there were no trade, oranges would be enormously less valuable relatively to ice in Jaffa than at the North Pole. In the same way copper would be enormously less valuable relatively to tin in a region containing copper mines but no tin mines than in one containing tin mines but no copper mines. Again, even though, in both of two regions, the same *kinds* of natural resources exist, the comparative *quantities* may differ. Thus, in one region, A, there is a much larger stock of agricultural land relatively to labour power or equipment than in another region, B ; or there is a much larger stock of unskilled manual labour power relatively to equipment than in B ; or there is a much larger stock of mental labour of medium quality relatively to skilled manual labour than in B ; and so on. Usually those kinds of productive resources which are relatively abun-

dant in any region will also be relatively cheap (in terms
of anything we choose) in that region. Hence, with
similar techniques and similar scales of output, in regions
where any given kind of productive resource is relatively
abundant the values of things in whose manufacture
that resource plays a large part, as compared with those
in regard to which it plays a small part, will be lower than
they are in other regions. For example, in the absence of
trade, the comparative values of chemicals and scientific
goods would be lower relatively to other things in Germany
than in the United States, because the German educational
system produces a great number of chemists. In the same
way in a country in which capital is abundant and the rate
of interest, therefore, low, things produced by industries
in which capital plays a large part would, in the absence
of trade, have a lower value, relatively to things made
chiefly by hand, than in other countries. But this is not
all. Even when two countries are closely similar as
regards productive resources, it will still very likely happen
that one of them specialises in one sort of product and the
other in another. If that happens, in each of them the
comparative value, as compared with other things, of
the thing in which it specialises is sure to be lower than
in the others. For all these reasons it is to be expected
that in the absence of trade there will be very considerable
differences in the comparative values of different things
in different countries.

Whenever this is so, provided that the differences in
comparative values are large enough to outweigh the
expenses of transport, trade will tend to take place ; and
each country will get the things that it imports with less
effort than it would have cost to make them for itself.
In effect, the opening up of opportunities for foreign trade
to any country enables the people of that country to
substitute a more economical method — the indirect
method of making and exchanging something else — for

the less economical method of direct manufacture. It is thus similar in general effect to the development of a technical improvement. Like that, it enlarges the country's income-getting power, and so, in general, its income. This is what Mill says about that : " The only direct advantage in foreign commerce consists in the imports. A country obtains things which it either could [or would] not have produced at all, or which it must have produced at a greater expense of capital and labour than the cost of things [in terms of capital and labour] which it exports to pay for them."[1] This may be compared with Marshall's statement : " The *prima facie* gain, which a country derives from her foreign trade, consists in the excess in the value to her of the things which she imports over the value to her of the things which she could [and would] have made for herself in their place ; *i.e.* with the amounts of capital and labour devoted to producing the things which she exported in exchange for them ; the costs of working the trade being, of course, reckoned in ".[2]

An important qualification or, rather, explanation has to be added. When opportunities for foreign trade are opened up and conditions are such that it pays people to make use of them, *for the time being* a country's income-getting power must be larger than it would have been without these opportunities. But the phrase *for the time being* is important. The immediate and direct effect of the opening up of foreign trade must be advantageous — the immediate and direct effect of obstructions to trade disadvantageous. But immediate and direct effects are not always the whole effects. In certain cases the opening up of foreign trade may do indirect and slow-working damage to a country's income-getting power, that in the long run more than offsets the immediate benefit. In such cases,

---

[1] *Principles of Political Economy*, vol. ii, p. 119 : I have inserted the words in square brackets.

[2] *Industry and Trade*, p. 17 : words in square brackets inserted by me.

D

by putting obstacles in the way of foreign trade, a country, though it would sacrifice income-getting power at the moment, would gain on the whole, because it would be building up income-getting power in the future. This is a central idea in Friederic List's argument for protecting infant industries in undeveloped countries. He writes : " The building up of manufacturing power, involving, as it does, the training of workmen, the perfecting of machinery, of transport and of market organisation, is a work of years ".[1] Till it has been completed, the old-established manufacturing State has " a thousand advantages over the newly born or half-grown manufacturers of other nations ".[2] In the natural course of things it will not be possible for younger rivals to grow up. Private individuals cannot face the risk and expenditure required to raise them from infancy to manhood. In such cases to the younger country foreign trade is, no doubt, immediately and directly advantageous ; but against the direct gain there has to be set a loss, in the fact that industries to which the natural conditions of that country are well adapted are prevented from developing. Moreover, this sort of indirect loss is not necessarily found only in connection with new countries. It may attach to portions of the foreign trade of a country that is industrially old. For even in an old country there are likely to be *some* new industries, for which the country is well fitted ultimately but in which it cannot compete effectively at the moment. Still this extension of List's infant industry argument is not very important for practice. The reason is that in an old country there will be an artisan class to draw from already trained ; banks and moneyed men to lend for distant returns ; and so on. This means that, in an old country, an industry for which that country is well adapted will usually be able to establish itself after a while on its own merits without the help of

[1] *A National System of Political Economy*, p. 319.　　[2] *Ibid.*, p. 300.

State-provided crutches. For such a country, therefore — England, for example — the qualification that I have been stating does not amount to much. Broadly speaking, the opening up of opportunities for foreign trade increases income-getting power in the same way that technical improvements do.

Of course, it does not follow that to obstruct foreign trade, for example, by high duties on particular imports, is always a mistake. Income-getting power is not the only thing that matters. For social or military reasons a country may want to have a large agricultural population. Or it may want to have certain key products — dyes, magnetos, optical glass — made at home, so as to insure against the risk of having the sources of their supply cut off in time of war. In order to satisfy these requirements it may be worth its while to obstruct permanently certain sorts of imports in spite of the fact that to do that cuts down its income-getting power. This sort of issue is political and outside the scope of economics.

So far I have been concerned with the relation of foreign dealings to a country's income-getting power in very general terms. For the remainder of this chapter I shall pass to something more limited and concrete — the particular foreign trade situation which this country will have to meet now that this war has ended. About that many people are very seriously concerned. The crucial point is this. On the average of 1936–8 we had annual claims on foreigners amounting to some £200 millions a year as interest on investments — about 5 per cent of our total annual income ; and we brought the whole of this in in the form of imports, not leaving any of it to be reinvested abroad. During the war not only has a substantial part of our foreign securities been sold, but we have also, apart altogether from Lease-Lend arrangements, contracted an enormous foreign debt — some £3000 millions. Instead, therefore, of being a creditor country for interest from foreigners, we may even be a debtor country on income account. We certainly shall not be a creditor country to the extent of anything like £200 millions' worth of stuff at pre-war value.

But to set out our post-war foreign trade situation in those terms is greatly to understate the difficulties with which we are likely to be faced. To realise properly what these are it is not enough to look at the quantity of stuff that we used to bring in from abroad as interest. We have to take into account the *detailed character* of the stuff that we used to import — of *all* this stuff, whether obtained by way of interest or by other means. The significance of foreign dealings for us depends on how they affect not merely the quantity but also the quality content of our real income.

Let me summarise the position. Before the war, apart from the great slump, something of the order of one-fifth of our productive resources were normally engaged in providing goods and services for export. As we have just seen, some £200 millions' worth of imports used to come in, not as payment for current exports, but as interest on investments made in the past. In the result something like one-fourth of the total value of our real income was made up of imports : a fraction naturally much larger than the corresponding fraction for the great continental areas of the United States and Russia. But that is only quantity. Now for quality. Before the war our exports consisted chiefly of manufactured goods, coal, the services of ships rendered to foreigners, and the services of bankers, commission houses and so on performed for them. Our imports, on the other hand, consisted in the main of food and raw materials for our industries. There were, of course, other things — some of them luxury goods like diamonds and expensive motor-cars ; but food and raw materials were much the most important items. Here is a passage from the Report of

44

the Balfour Committee on Industry and Trade. Though it is now nearly twenty years old, it gives an excellent general picture of the facts. " During the forty years, 1881 to 1921, the population of Great Britain increased by 13 millions, or about 43 per cent, and during that period the proportion of the occupied population engaged in agriculture fell from over 12 per cent to about 7 per cent. In 1927 the value of our net imports of food and raw materials amounted to nearly £800 millions. About four-fifths of our supply of wheat and flour and three-fifths of our supply of meat came from abroad. Coal is the only important raw material in which Great Britain is self-supporting. The whole of the cotton, nine-tenths of the wool and timber, and more than a third of the iron ore which we use are imported from overseas."[1] Now food and raw material are fundamental and essential things. The country would suffer enormously more if its supplies of these goods were cut down by so many million pounds' worth than if the supplies of goods in general were cut down by an equal amount. In short, the special character of the goods we chiefly receive through foreign dealings makes these dealings a much more important factor in our economy than the mere aggregate value of them, large though that is, suggests when taken by itself. It is not merely that our income-getting power is threatened with a cut of, say, from 3 to 5 per cent *in a general way*, but with that cut made *in a specially sensitive place*.

Bearing this in mind, consider these more detailed figures. On the average of the years 1936–8 our annual imports other than those intended for immediate re-export amounted to £866 millions. Against these we exported

Merchandise	£478 millions
Shipping services	105 „
Bankers' services, etc.	40 „

[1] *Loc. cit.*, Final Report, p. 8.

45

making £623 millions altogether. The adverse balance
of £243 millions was met, to the extent of £203 millions,
out of interest due to us on British-held foreign securities,
and, to the extent of £40 millions, by borrowing. In
trying to forecast what the position is likely to be in the
future, we need not speculate about probable changes
in general price levels. It is the real situation in terms of
goods and services that matters. So I shall speak in
terms of pre-war, not post-war, prices. Let us take it, then,
for a guess that our net interest claims have been reduced
to a quarter of what they were ; so that we have £150
millions' worth less of current receipts (at pre-war values)
with which to pay for imports. Owing to the special
character of the things we get from abroad we cannot
simply drop that value of imports, but must try to shift the
income-getting power that remains to us in such a way as
still to bring in a good part of them. We are thus faced,
not merely with a loss, but also with a problem.

Suppose, by way of illustration, that we are determined
to import as much as before. If our shipping and banking
services to foreigners are unchanged, it seems at first
sight, that, in order to do this without resort to more
extensive borrowing, we should have to increase our
exports of merchandise by £150 millions' worth at pre-
war prices, that is, by some 30 per cent. But the situation
is really worse than this. On the average, our pre-war
exports of merchandise consisted, to the extent of about
37 per cent, of imported raw and other materials.[1] In order,
therefore, to get in balance after the war it would not be
enough to increase our exports of merchandise by £150
millions at pre-war prices. We should need also to buy
from abroad the foreign materials to be embodied in the
extra exports. That is, we should need to increase *total*
exports of merchandise, including their import content,
not by £150 millions but by £150 millions multiplied by

[1] Schumacher, *Export Policy and Full Employment*, p 7.

46

$\frac{100}{63}$, nearly £240 millions; not in fact by 30 per cent but by more like 45 per cent.

This is on the assumption that we still render to foreigners about as much shipping and banking services as we did before the war. But during the course of the war, our merchant shipping fleet has been greatly reduced, while that of the United States has been greatly expanded. That makes it very unlikely that we shall be able to earn so much from foreigners in real terms by means of these services as we used to do. Moreover, if the widely held hopes of better employment after the war are fulfilled, our wage-earners as a body, being better off, will want more food. That means still more imports. In view of these things it is often claimed that, to get square with the new situation on pre-war lines, we shall need to export in physical quantities half as much merchandise again as we exported in the last three pre-war years. This is on the assumption that increase of our exports is not accompanied by any decrease in the purchasing power of these exports in terms of imports. If it is, the increase in exports will have to be still larger. In my opinion, indeed, the guess that a 50 per cent increase will be needed, which, by politicians and journalists, now seems to be regarded as a statistically established fact, may well prove an underestimate. Still, for want of something better, let us adopt it. It is a large enough figure to make it plain that our situation will be a difficult one.

There are two ways in which at once the drop in our income-getting power may be partly made good and also our special import-export problem partly solved. The first is this. Through improvements in technique and organisation, we may become more efficient in producing goods that foreigners would like to buy from us. This would enable us to offer these goods more cheaply in terms of foreign goods and consequently to sell more of them. It *might* happen that, in consequence of the increased supply, the prices of our exports in terms of imports would fall more than in proportion to the expansion of exports ; so that the larger volume of these bought less, not more, imports than before. In that case, of course, we should be worse, not better off. But there is a strong presumption that an increase in our exports on account of improved efficiency would not reduce the value of them per unit in anything like an equivalent proportion ; so that, though a 50 per cent increase in our exports brought about in this way would not yield a 50 per cent increase in the imports exchanged against them, it would yield something not very far short of that. *Pro tanto* our loss of income-getting power would be made good and our special import-export problem solved.

Secondly, the foreign demand schedule for our exports may be substantially raised, with the result both that a unit of these exports buys more imports and also that we are able to sell more exports. Here, indeed, we start in a weak position. During the war our exports of merchandise to the neutral world have necessarily been much cut down. In consequence, a number of foreign countries will have learnt to make for themselves the kinds of goods that they used to take from us and so will be worse customers for our exports than they used to be. Still, though there will be leeway to make up, that does not rule out an eventual — possibly an early — expansion of foreign demand for our exports above the pre-war level. This may come about in several ways. After the 1914–18 war the purchasing power of our exports in terms of the foreign goods we wanted increased substantially, because agriculture had been greatly expanded in Canada and the United States on account of the war, and, consequently, agricultural goods — our chief import — were very abundant and cheap. Indeed, they became so cheap that we were able to get all the imports we wanted with *less* exports than before ; and this fact was probably responsible, at least in part, for the depressed state of our export industries in the earlier inter-war years. An expansion in foreign demand for our exports might also come about through improvements in general prosperity, and so real purchasing power, in foreign countries ; or through a reduction in foreign tariffs affecting our goods ; or through the removal of the many different kinds of obstacles that in the years immediately before the war governments were putting in the way of foreign trade. It is sometimes thought that the foreign demand for our exports could also be enhanced if we contrived to make discriminatory trade treaties favourable to ourselves with countries against whom we are in a strong bargaining position. Here, however, there is a risk of economic warfare. We might easily, on the whole, do ourselves more harm than good. But that is a secondary matter. In a general way it is clear that an expansion in the foreign demand for our exports, like an improvement in the technique of our export industries, would *pro tanto* both make good our loss of income-getting power and also solve our special import-export problem.

Should these two remedial processes fall short of what is needed, that special import-export problem might be met, though our loss of income-getting power could not be made good, by increased annual borrowing from abroad. It is sometimes thought that such borrowing necessarily entails living on our capital, and is to be condemned on that ground. This is a mistake. To borrow £150 millions a year abroad does not entail living on our capital, provided that at the same time we are annually creating more than £150 millions' worth of new capital at home. In the years preceding this war we were in fact borrowing from abroad, but, none the less, increasing our total capital stock every year. Foreign borrowing in peace-time, even for a developed country such as this, is not necessarily a thing to frown on. But, if it is practised on at all a big scale, foreign debt piles up very quickly, and, the bigger the debt, the more difficult further borrowing becomes. It is very unlikely that this device can contribute seriously for more than a short time towards solving our post-war import-export problem.

The alternative is a reduction in the scale of our imports — cutting our coat to match our cloth. This can be accomplished in either of two ways : by dispensing with some of the things we used to import, or by making them at home instead of importing them. Since by far the greater part of our imports are food and raw materials, we cannot easily, except for a comparatively small volume of luxuries, dispense with them. In so far as the import-export gap has to be closed by cutting down imports, we shall have for the most part to make for ourselves the goods we used to import as payment of interest on our foreign investments. This would mean, among other things, an extension of home agriculture substantially beyond its pre-war scale The disappearance of our annual interest from abroad, so far as that is not offset by other things, will of itself automatically create a tendency towards this. For, owing to the shortage of competing imports, farming here will be a more profitable industry. Some sort of adjustment will, therefore, take place, even though the Government does nothing at all about it. But this adjustment might be of a kind to raise the real cost of food seriously, and so to lower the standard of living of the poorer classes. If that happens, the Government will very likely have to continue its war-time policy of food subsidies. Nobody will want the damage done by our loss of income-getting power to fall with special severity upon those members of the community who are least able to sustain it.

CHAPTER IV

THE ALLOCATION OF INCOME-GETTING POWER AMONG DIFFERENT SORTS OF PRODUCTION

THE people of this country expend their money income on different sorts of goods and services in certain definite proportions. The White Paper published on behalf of the Chancellor of the Exchequer in April 1944 estimated that personal expenditure on consumption, excluding indirect taxes, amounted in 1938, the last complete year before the war, to some £3500 millions out of a net national income of some £4600 millions, that is, to about three-fourths of the whole. This personal expenditure was divided up as follows. Food, drink and tobacco absorbed about 39 per cent; rent, rates, fuel, lighting and other household goods 24½ per cent; clothes, 11 per cent; these items together coming to just about three-quarters of all personal expenditure on consumption. It is of interest to notice that travel, including travel by motor, accounted for about 7 per cent. Some estimates made earlier by private investigators go into greater detail. One writer, for example, found that the curious admixture, 'Religion, Reading and Miscellaneous', accounted for 6¼ per cent of aggregate expenditure, say 5 per cent of expenditure on personal consumption. But I shall not go further into that.

It might be thought at first sight that, from the analysis of the way in which expenditure is allocated among different things, we could directly infer the way in which the country's productive resources are devoted to making different things. If the country were perfectly self-contained, this would, of course, be so. But in fact the things on which people spend income are not all made at home. As we saw in the last chapter, some of them are imported in exchange for different sorts of home-made goods that are exported. Thus a great deal of our food is paid for by the exports of British manufactured goods and coal, the services of British ships and so on. The resources which produce these things are, in effect, producing food for us in an indirect roundabout way. This implies that the proportion of our resources engaged directly in producing food at home is very much less than the proportion of our national income that is spent on food. We must not, therefore, use statistics of the proportions in which the country's money income is spent on different things as a measure of the proportions in which our resources are allocated to the direct production of these different things. We must look at what happens to productive resources without this kind of mediation.

Now these resources, as we have seen, fall into three main groups, Land, Capital and Labour. For the two first groups detailed statistics about allocation among uses are not easily available. But for the third group, Labour, we have a good deal of information ; and about that I shall say a little. Statistics collected in connection with unemployment insurance cover some of the ground, but the most recent full-scale account, covering all of it, is in the Census Report of 1931. An important section of that Report is devoted to an 'industrial classification' of the people of the country. This is to be distinguished from an 'occupational' classification. In that each man is entered under his craft or work irrespective of its ultimate purpose, so that all carpenters, wherever employed, are classed together. In an industrial classification, on the other hand each person is entered under the industry of his employer, so that carpenters engaged by a railway company are entered under railways. It is the industrial classification of the 1931 Census that provides the material I am going to use.

There is a preliminary difficulty. What principles are available for building an industrial classification and how are they actually used in our census ? From the standpoint of anybody wanting to make a description it would be very convenient if each industry consisted of one or more firms, each making one precisely definable commodity and nothing else. But, of course, in actual life that doesn't happen. Pretty well everything that we ordinarily think of either as an industry or as a firm is engaged in making a large variety of different commodities ; and sometimes a firm may be engaged in making things so very different, for example chocolates and wooden boxes in which to pack them, that it may seem, so to speak, to belong to two or more industries. We are clearly already faced with troubles about definition.

Several methods or principles of classification can be used. One method is to take as a basis the broad purpose that various things serve. Thus we might group industries under the main heads, food, clothes, houses, furniture and so on. Each of these main groups might be further subdivided according to the purposes that the things contained in it chiefly serve. Thus under clothes we might have head-gear, foot-gear, underwear, outer wear ; under furniture, bedroom furniture, kitchen furniture, sitting-room furniture ; under vehicles, cars, carts, trams, buses ; and so on. A second method is to separate off broad groups according to the material used. Thus we might have industries making cotton goods, woollen goods, iron and steel goods, chemicals and so on. A third method is to group industries according to the process employed ; for example, building, including shipbuilding ; weaving, covering all sorts of textiles ; mining, covering all sorts of mining.

In the actual classifications of our census all these principles, purpose, material and process, are used — the census authorities following as closely as they conveniently can customary ways of speech and thought. Those people are classified as belonging to the same industry who, for one reason or another, think they do so. This is excellently put by Mr. Austin Robinson in a passage that I will quote : " In practice all that we can do is to follow the example of those who are actually engaged in industries. Certain employers find that they have a common bond of interest with certain other employers and come to regard themselves as composing an industry. The bond may be one of the broad type of general product, as in the motor industry, the electrical industry, the paper-box industry. It may be one of a common use of a single raw material, as in the iron and steel industry, the pottery industry, the cotton industry It may be one of a common use of a given type of machinery or a given process of manufacture. Thus we may distinguish the textile industries ; we may speak of brass-founders or of steel-rolling firms as having something in common which distinguishes them from other firms. Industries as such have no identity. They are simply a classification of firms, which may for the moment be convenient. A change of technique or of organisation may require a new classification and a new industry." [1]

Now for the facts. In 1931 the number of persons in England and Wales gainfully occupied was 18,853,000, about 10 per cent more than in 1921. This 10 per cent increase compares with an increase in the total population of $5\frac{1}{2}$ per cent. The reason for the difference is that, owing to the fall in the birth rate, the proportion of persons of working age was much larger. In 1931 the proportion of males over 14 returned as occupied was 83 per cent; of females over 14, 34·2 per cent

The 18,853,000 persons gainfully occupied, whether on the day of the census they were out of work or not, were grouped in industries as follows :

[1] E. A. G. Robinson, *The Structure of Competitive Industry*, pp. 12-13

	Per cent	
Manufactures of all kinds	39·0	}
Agriculture and fishing	5·7	} 50·7
Mining and quarrying	6·0	}
Commerce	15·8	}
Transport and communication	6·8	} 22·6
Personal service, including hotels	12·8	
Public administration	6·5	
Professions	3·1	
Defence	1·3	
Gas, water, electricity	1·0	
Entertainments, sports, odds and ends	1·8	

The largest grouping in this list, 39 per cent for manufactures of all kinds, is further subdivided as follows :

	Per cent
Metals, machinery, etc.	11·6
Textiles	6·3
Building and decoration	6·0
Clothing	5·4
Food, drink and tobacco	3·3
Others	8·3

Let us now turn from facts and estimates to explanations. By what influences and in what manner is it brought about that the working population of a country is allocated among different occupations in the way in which at any time it is allocated ; and how are the differences between the ways in which it is allocated at different times accounted for ? This is a very far-reaching problem, and an important section of economics is devoted to exploring it. My chief purpose in this chapter is to attempt an outline sketch of the answer.

In times of war, as everybody knows, the allocation of people of working age to various sorts of work is predominantly determined by authoritative action on the part of the Government, not by individual choice. People are conscripted for the Armed Forces and directed to this or that kind of civilian work. Moreover, even when authority does not act directly, it often acts indirectly, by limiting the supplies of raw materials to industries the scale of which it wishes to cut down ; and so on. In these conditions, though, of course, the practical problems that have to be faced are large and very serious, there is no problem for general economic analysis. People are allocated as they are allocated because the Government so orders them. It says unto this man, " Go," and he goeth ; and there is nothing more to be said by anybody else

But in normal times in what we may call free communities everything is quite different. It may be that, for a year or two out of their lives, men are conscripted for compulsory military training — though in England and the United States before 1939 this did not happen in peace-time. But the great mass of the people are not sent into particular jobs by Government order. Their allocation among jobs and industries is not settled in that simple straightforward way. How, then, is it settled ? People choose their own jobs or their parents choose them for them. What lies behind this multitude of independent individual choices ? Why is the number of motor mechanics what it is and not ten times or one-tenth as large ? What are the forces that govern the arrangement of the bricks in our economic structure ; and how do these forces work ? There are two principal sets of influences which economists find it convenient to distinguish under the two broad headings, Supply and Demand. I shall first speak about Supply influences separately, then about Demand influences separately and, after that, about the way in which the two sets are interlocked.

Under the head of Supply consider first a number of men, all of the same quality and capacity, confronted with a number of different opportunities for employment in various places and various jobs. If the net advantages obtained from work in one place or job are markedly greater than those obtained in another, they will tend to move away from the second towards the first. For naturally they want to get the best return for their efforts that they can. There will be a tendency for them to shift about in this way so long as there is any difference between the net advantages obtainable in different places and jobs. As the numbers offering themselves at the more favoured openings grow, the rate of pay to be had there consequently falls. Conversely, as men move away from the less favoured openings, scarcity of labour makes itself felt there and the rate of pay rises. In this way it comes about that the numbers of men offering their services in different places and jobs tend to be so adjusted that the net advantages obtainable in any one of them are the same or nearly the same as those obtainable in any other. Adam Smith puts the point in this way : " The whole of the advantages and disadvantages of the different employments of labour and stock must in the same neighbourhood be either perfectly equal or continually tending to equality. If in the same neighbourhood there was any employment evidently either more or less advantageous than the rest, so many people would crowd into it in the one case and so many would desert it in the other that its advantages would soon return to the level of other employments. This at least would be the case in a Society where things were left to follow their natural course, where there was perfect liberty and where every man was perfectly free both to choose what occupation he thought proper and to change it as often as he thought proper." [1] This general principle on the side of Supply can be, as it has been, set out very shortly. But, in order that its practical significance may be understood, some explanations and elaborations must be added.

Thus we have to be on guard against mistakes arising from the fact that different things are often described

[1] *Wealth of Nations* (Scott's edition), vol. i, p. 101.

under the same name. Within any calling of a given name there are bound to be persons of very different capacity. There is no tendency for 'boxers', only for boxers of similar grades, to get the same pay in different places. As Lord Pethick-Lawrence showed in an excellent book on *Local Variations of Wages*, written nearly half a century ago, many variations that at first sight seemed puzzling are found on detailed investigation to be accounted for along these lines.

Next we have to unravel some complications in the notion 'equal net advantages'. First, equality of net advantages is not necessarily secured to similar men in the sense here intended if they get equal net advantages per piece of work done — equal piece wages. Different men may be engaged with machines of different quality or they may be getting different amounts of help from the management. Equal piece wages have no *prima facie* tendency to carry equal net advantages in my sense to similar men when these men are employed in dissimilar conditions. Secondly, equality of net advantages in different occupations and places is not necessarily secured when the net advantages obtained against an hour's work or a day's work, or a week's work, or even a year's work of given intensity are equal. Account must be taken of the fact that in some occupations work is available more regularly and, perhaps, for a larger part of a man's life than in others.

Thus equal net advantages per day's work are not equal net advantages in our sense as between, say, dockers on casual work and railwaymen who may reckon on firm employment all the year round. Again, in some jobs a man may reckon on a longer working life than in others. A ping-pong champion is past his best at 18, a boxer or a sprinter in the early 20's, a long-distance runner by the time he is 30. When Big Bill Tilden, the celebrated lawn-tennis player, was 38, the newspapers began to shake

their heads and talk of him as a veteran. In more intellectual fields mathematicians and artists are often at their
best in early life. Historians ripen later. Masters at
Eton are superannuated at 57 ; Cambridge Professors at
65 ; Heads of Colleges at 70 — unless by a special vote
it is decided to let one of them jog along till 75. Politicians, on the other hand, are headstrong youths at 50,
about fit for high office at 65, still going strong at 80.
It is not till they have tipped the century that the leader
of their Party whispers : " Old So-and-so is getting a bit
hard of hearing ; in another ten years we shall have to
make him a Judge " Yet again, you must allow for the
fact that some jobs are blind alleys, while others are
stepping-stones to higher things. Errand-boys have to
have high wages because they sacrifice the chance of
learning a trade. Parliamentary private secretaries to
Ministers, on the other hand, are glad to serve for no
wages at all, because in that way they are introduced to
the political limelight, to the prospects of what a recent
Lord Chancellor, once known to fame as Galloper Smith,
called 'the glittering prizes of life'.

Thirdly, to descend from poetry to prose, one has to
bear in mind that the net advantages of various occupations, though they often bear a close relation to money
wages, are not exactly represented by them. In some jobs
there are necessary outgoings, wigs for Judges, gowns
for University Dons (except in the Engineering Labora-
tories), that are a partial set-off to the money wages.
In others there are incidental extras — the perquisites of
bed-makers, the free coal of some coal-miners, the free
cider or beer, or even cottages, of some agricultural
labourers. Then there are social amenities and dis-
amenities. To be a clergyman is — in some quarters —
highly thought of ; to be a hangman is not. Therefore
for equal net advantages a hangman must have more pay.

It would be easy to go on elaborating these qualifications and elucidations. But they do not affect the main principle. This, to repeat, is simply that among people of similar capacity, if those engaged in making bicycles are better off than those engaged in making hats, some hat-makers will drift across into making bicycles until the prospects of both jobs are alike and there is no inducement towards further drifting. Of course, adjustment won't be made instantly. After a big disturbance it may well be that quite large disparities of earnings among similar men in different jobs and places continue for a long time. But the *tendency* to adjustment, however delayed or obstructed, is always there. The motive force at work is simply the general desire to get as good wages as one can.

So far I have been talking about people of similar qualities. But the general principle which I have been describing under the head of Supply extends further than this. Let us, so as not to lose the wood in the trees, ignore the fact of different inborn qualities and suppose that all babies are born alike. Even so, when grown up, they may have different actual qualities, on account of differences in their training and education. For a rough approximation these differences may be looked at as the result of different kinds and quantities of investment made in them. It is easy to see then that the general principle I have been describing must so work that there is a tendency for investment to be pushed into creating different sorts of capacity in such proportions that £100 invested in training one man for one kind of capacity yields, or rather is expected to yield, the same return as £100 invested in training another man for another kind. Hence, when different sorts of skill entail about equal investments in training, there will be a tendency for people to be trained for different occupations in such proportions that their rates of pay are about equal — for example, different sorts of artisans; grooms and chauffeurs;

lecturers in mathematics and lecturers in classics. Of course, the adjustment is extremely imperfect. One obvious reason is that investment has often to be made a long time ahead. If schoolmasters in mathematics now are getting more pay than schoolmasters in classics, that tends to make people invest in learning mathematics rather than classics ; and that in turn tends, by increasing the number of mathematical schoolmasters, to bring down their pay nearer to that of classical schoolmasters. But it takes a long time to train a mathematician. Before the extra investment has taken effect the relative demands for the two sorts of schoolmasters may have altered a great deal, with the result that the extra investment in mathematicians does *not* in fact lead to the number of them being what would be required to bring about equal pay. There is a tendency that way, but it may easily fail to be realised.

There is yet a further application of my general Supply principle. Consider the allocation of people among occupations that require *different* amounts of investment in training — unskilled labourers, artisans, clerks, highly trained doctors or lawyers. Here the tendency will clearly not be to an allocation that entails equal pay, but rather to one that entails differences of pay more or less corresponding to the differences in the amounts of investment needed. If the excess of pay to be got as an artisan as compared with an unskilled labourer is too little for this, people will be dissuaded from having their children trained as artisans ; and so on generally over the whole range of occupations. But here the adjustment is bound to be even more imperfect than it is for occupations in all of which the training needed costs about the same. The reason is this. For occupations that require very expensive training boys can only be trained if their fathers are well-to-do or if they get help from scholarship grants. This may entail — and, apart from scholarship grants, it certainly will entail — that investment in these occupations is strongly obstructed. This means that the tendency for rates of pay in these expensive occupations only to differ from the rates in others in correspondence with the extra investment required in them is largely frustrated. Rates of pay there will be too high ; the number of people allocated there too few. The Supply principle here moves on a very broken wing.

To sum up these influences. Men of similar inborn quality — and here, in Churchillian phrase, ' man embraces woman ' — being anxious to do as well for themselves and their families as they can, tend so to allocate themselves among occupations that nobody would gain by shifting out of the occupation where he is into another one. This entails that net advantages — roughly the rates of pay — tend to be similar in different occupations for kinds of work that require equally expensive training; and, where the work of one occupation needs more training than that of another, to be higher in the former in a degree more or less corresponding to the extra cost of training there. These tendencies only work themselves out very imperfectly and sometimes very slowly. They are the dominant factors on the Supply side affecting the way in which labour — and similar considerations apply to other productive agents — is allocated among different occupations.

Turn now to the Demand side. The fundamental thing here is that, at any given rate of wages, that number of men of given quality tends to be engaged by employers, and so allocated to any industry, which is demanded there, at that rate of wages. To develop this principle we must enquire what the influences are which decide how many such men will in fact be demanded in any industry at any given rate of wages. These influences can be grouped under three heads : first, and most obviously, the state of public demand for the particular kind or kinds of goods that the industry produces ; secondly, the relation between the number of work-people employed and the quantity of their output ; thirdly, the conditions, competitive or monopolistic, under which their output is sold. It would take too long to elaborate the analysis that lies behind these summary sentences. But it is worth while to illustrate some of the things implied in it.

First, the demand price for any given quantity of labour of given quality will be larger, and therefore, at any given rate of wages, more labour will be wanted in any industry, the keener people in general are for the products of that industry. If ladies who used to like hairpins come to like lipstick instead, more men will presently be found making lipstick and fewer making hairpins.

Secondly, on the same principle, more labour will be wanted in any industry, the better-to-do are the people who care about the product of that industry ; because, of course, a very keen desire by a poor man leads to the purchase of much less of anything than quite a mild desire by a rich man. If, then, people who like beer become twice as well-to-do as they used to be and people who like cider half as well-to-do, there will presently be more men making beer and fewer making cider.

Thirdly, what is the effect on the number of work-people wanted in and allocated to an industry if, through improved methods and so on, a unit of labour comes to produce more stuff ? To this question there is not a single yes-and-no answer. In some conditions the effect will be to increase, in others to decrease, the number of work-people wanted in the industry at a given rate of wages. If people's demand for the product is very inelastic, that is to say, if a considerable cheapening of it makes very little difference to the quantity they want, increased productive efficiency will enable them to get all they want by the use of less labour than before. On the other hand, if the demand for the product is very elastic, so that a very slight cheapening will make a large difference to the quantity that they want, they will ask for so much more product than before that more, and not less, labour will be allocated to it, in spite of the fact that each unit of labour is producing more stuff than before. In a general way, we may expect that increased efficiency in industries producing necessaries will cause less labour to be engaged in them, while increased efficiency in industries producing luxuries will cause more labour to be engaged there.

Fourthly, if any article is being produced under competitive conditions, employers will hire labour to produce it up to that point at which the selling price of the last unit produced just balances the wages of the work-people — I am ignoring other agents of production — needed to make it. For example, if a unit of labour during a day makes two units of some product, the price of the product tends to be equal to half the workman's daily wage. But, if conditions of monopoly exist, it will pay employers to cut down their output so as to raise prices. In consequence the price of the produce will be more than half a worker's daily wage; less of it will be bought by the public; less produced; and less labour engaged in making it. The introduction of monopolistic practices into any industry means then that less labour is wanted in and allocated to that industry than would be allocated to it if it were being conducted in competitive conditions.

I have now to try to make clear the relation between what I have just been saying from the side of Demand and what I said earlier from the side of Supply. Somebody perhaps may be thinking that I started off by giving an explanation of the allocation of labour among industries from the one side and then crossed over and gave quite a different one from the other. That is not so. It is impossible to give an explanation from either side taken by itself. This can easily be shown. Supply influences decide that such numbers of men of given quality will tend to be allocated to different occupations as are required to make the net advantages — wage rates and so on — to be got in all of them about the same. But they do not decide what the numbers that are required to do this are. For example, if the public are very keen on bicycles and only mildly keen on hats, for wages to be held the same in bicycle-making and in hat-making there will have to be a lot of people working on bicycles and only a few on hats. But, if people change their tastes and come to want few bicycles and many hats, for wages to be held the same in the two jobs there will have to be only a few people working on bicycles and a lot working on hats. Thus the influences on the supply side taken by themselves cannot determine how labour will be allocated among occupations. On the other side, demand influences decide that in any occupation, when any given wage rate is ruling, the number of men allocated to it will be such as to make the demand price in respect of that number equal to the wage rate. But they decide nothing about what the wage rates in the several occupations will be or how they will be related to one another. These influences, therefore, by themselves, like supply influences by themselves, cannot determine how labour will be allocated among occupations. For that both sets of influences are needed. That is to say, the allocation of labour among industries is determined, not by supply conditions alone or by demand conditions alone, but by the interplay of both sets of conditions.

To make this finally clear, suppose that we start with a situation in which there are X men of given quality engaged in hat-making and Y men in bicycle-making. Then, as I showed at the bottom of p. 62, the wages of men in hat-making will be equal to the demand price per unit of X men there and the wages of men in bicycle-making to the demand price per unit of Y men there.

65

This satisfies the demand side conditions. But if, as a result of this, a man of given quality can earn more at bicycle-making than at hat-making, men will tend to move from hats to bicycles, and to go on moving until equality is established. In this way the supply side conditions are satisfied. But this does not mean that the demand side conditions are not satisfied any longer; that the men in the two industries are not now paid their demand prices. For, as numbers change, the demand prices for the new numbers become different from what they were for the old. People have moved in such a way that, while rates of pay are still equal to demand prices everywhere, these demand prices themselves have been modified by shifts in numbers so as to fit in with a further equality — equality of rates of pay to men of similar quality or similar capacity — with appropriate differences for men of dissimilar qualities, in all industries. Thus influences on the side of supply and influences on the side of demand *co-operate* in settling how labour shall be allocated among industries; just as, to borrow Marshall's illustration, the two blades of a pair of scissors co-operate in cutting cloth. Neither is before or after the other. They reign together in equal glory.

In all this discussion I have explicitly left out of account an important complication — the evident fact that different people come into the world with different inborn qualities. I do not mean by this merely that some persons are inherently more capable than others *all round*. That does not matter. If that were all, a person who was twice as capable as another, would simply count as equal to two of the other, getting twice as much pay whatever he did. Different men would simply contain, as it were, different numbers of units of labour, and every-thing that I have said so far could be adapted to this situation by substituting for the word 'person' the words 'unit of labour'. But in fact one person, whether as

66

regards inborn or finished quality, does not differ from another by being 10 or 20 or 50 per cent more or less capable all round. Human beings are not like certain types of crystals, all of exactly the same shape and differing only in size. They are of different shapes ; in the sense that for one type of work Jones may be 50 per cent more capable than Smith, for another type 20 per cent more capable, for another 5 per cent more capable, for another 20 or 30 per cent less capable. This fact makes it necessary to extend a little the analysis so far carried out.

Suppose that there are r different kinds of work and q different types of persons, each endowed with different *relative* capacities for the several kinds of work. Competition tends to bring it about that, for a unit of any kind of work, the same rate of pay is handed over, no matter by what type of person it is provided ; so that, among people doing a given kind of work, a man who is twice as capable as another gets twice as much pay. Moreover, the total quantity of each kind of work that is performed must be such that the demand price for that quantity is equal to the wage rate per unit for that kind of work. This we have already agreed. We have now to add something further. No person of any type will engage himself in a kind of work that would yield to him less pay than he could get by devoting himself to a different kind : — just as in equilibrium no piece of land will be devoted to wheat-growing which would earn more as pasture. It follows that the sets of relative capacities for different kinds of work with which people are born are an element, so far unnoticed in this discussion, which enters into the general body of supply conditions. In this way it helps, along with influences on the side of demand, to determine at once the numbers of people offering for different kinds of work, the rates of pay per piece for these different kinds, and the comparative wage rates per week of persons endowed with different sets of relative capacities. The whole body of relevant influences can be conveniently brought together in a system of mathematical equations.

What I have just been saying probably sounds academic and remote from reality. In fact it has a close bearing on a matter of wide current interest, the comparative weekly wage rates paid to men and women — something that is obviously interlocked very closely with the allocation of jobs between the two sexes. To show how this comes to be so, let us, for the purposes of the argument, ignore individual differences and make for ourselves a simplified model in which all men are alike — representative men — and all women are alike — representative women. We then get a special case of the general set-up that I have been describing, with the number of different sets of original relative endowments possessed by different people reduced to two instead of being a large number. Draw up in imagination a list of various kinds of work, iron puddling, coal-mining, typewriting, nursing and so on, and put down the number of units of work of each kind that a man can perform and that a woman can perform. We put at the top of the list the kind of work of which a man can perform the largest number of units, not necessarily in an absolute sense, but relatively to a woman ; next the one for which his relative performance is next greatest, and so on all down the list. In this model competition tends to secure that all men get the same wage and so also do all women. What determines the relative wages of men and women? If there is any kind of work in which both men and women are engaged — and we may suppose that there is some kind — the rate of pay per unit of work there must tend under the pressure of competition to be the same whether it is provided by a man or by a woman. In this sense, apart from friction, traditional prejudice and so on, equal pay for equal work tends — we must emphasise tends — to

be established. Since then, in our model all men's day
wages are the same and so also are all women's, men's day
wages everywhere bear to women's everywhere the same
ratio that men's capacities bear to women's capacities *in
that kind of work where both sexes are employed.* What
kind of work will that be ? — or rather, what place will
it occupy in the list of kinds that I have supposed to be
drawn up ?

The keener is the public demand for kinds of work
in which men's capacity relatively to women's is large,
and the smaller is the aggregate number of men offering
themselves for work, the less likely it is that any man
will be engaged in kinds of work in which men have
less capacity absolutely than women. Thus anything that
pushes up the demand for iron puddling, coal-mining and
so on makes it more likely that the marginal occupation
(or occupations) common to men and women will be one
in which men are more capable, and so earn more per
day. Any customary or legal regulations which exclude
women from occupations for which they are specially well
fitted has the same effect. On the other hand, anything
that pushes up the demand for such work as nursing, looking after young children and so on, for which women's
capacity is relatively large, makes it more likely that the
marginal occupation will be one in which women are more
capable, and so earn more per day. Again, anything that
reduces the number of men desiring work, for example
high war casualties, will make it more likely that the
marginal occupation will be one in which men are more
capable ; and anything that increases the number of women
desiring work, such as low earnings by their husbands
or readiness to accept low pay because, in general, the
man supports the family, will have the same effect. These
influences affect at one and the same time what the
marginal occupation or occupations engaging both men
and women (at equal piece wages) will be ; and also what

the relative rates of pay (time earnings) of representative men and representative women throughout all occupations will be. Of course, the tendencies thus set up are often interfered with by frictions, monopolistic pressures, prejudices and so on. But the tendencies are there, a sort of ground swell always beating against, though not necessarily always overcoming, superficial and, in a sense, accidental resistances.

For completeness one further comment should be added. In this analysis it has been tacitly assumed that the numbers of persons with different sets of inborn relative capacities are given independently of the rates of (weekly) wages that these several types of persons are respectively earning. With regard to men and women this is obviously true. The comparative number of boys and girls born and — except where infanticide is practised — reared is not dependent at all upon the comparative wages earned by members of the two sexes. But with qualities other than maleness and femaleness this is not so clear. For example, if giants or dwarfs are able to earn abnormally high wages, this may react on the size of their families, causing them to have more or, it may perhaps be, fewer, children than the average. There is — at all events let us suppose that there is — a greater chance that giants will have gigantic children and dwarfs dwarfish children than normal persons. To this extent, then, the wage rates earned by people with different sets of inborn qualities react on the numbers possessing the several sets of qualities ; and so a new complication is introduced. Obviously the reactions must take a long time to work themselves out. For this reason, though they may be important in the long run, they have not much bearing on short-period problems. There is no difficulty in taking account of them, if we want to, in a mathematical scheme embracing the whole situation.

CHAPTER V

THE RÔLE OF GOVERNMENT IN PRODUCTION

REAL income, as I have defined it, has no interest or importance in itself. It is significant only because of its bearing on the well-being of the people to whom it goes. This, by whatever name we may call it and whatever formal definition we may give to it, is the end ; income only a means to that end. There is a sentence by a French writer, which brings out this point very well : " In reality material objects are never more than the occasion or condition of economic facts ; the true economic facts are of the states of mind [*idées*] of men in relation to these objects ".[1] In this chapter, therefore, I shall go behind, not merely money income, but real income also, by-passing these things, so to speak, and going down to the relation between certain sorts of State action and general economic welfare. Fortunately it will not be necessary to go into subtleties about the exact meaning, or difficulties as regards the measurement, of that.

In any modern country there are certain functions bearing directly on economic life which Government authorities *must* perform, for the simple reason that nobody else *can* perform them. Thus Government must enact *some* laws, no matter what sort of laws, about property, contract, succession and currency —the institutions within which economic forces operate. Nor can it stop at enacting laws ; it must also enforce them. For this purpose it must maintain a system of law courts and a Police Force ; and, further, if there is any risk of aggression from foreigners, an Army, Navy and Air

[1] Seignobos, *La Méthode historique appliquée aux sciences sociales*, p. 113.

Force. Nobody else can do these things. They constitute the essential minimum of Government action. Of course, they entail a cost — a using-up of some of the productive resources of the community. For these resources Government authorities, even if they use conscription, must make payments ; and this means that they must raise taxes from their citizens to provide for the payments. All these considerable functions must be undertaken by governments even under a system of complete so-called *laissez-faire* — even if in economic matters they rigorously refuse to do more than keep the ring. This is the minimum of State action in economic affairs, and about it there is general agreement. But, over and above this, there are three important departments of economic life in which State action is widely advocated and has often been undertaken. These are, first, production, the ways in which real income is produced and resources allocated among different sorts of output ; secondly, the distribution of income over time ; thirdly, its distribution among people. In Chapters VI and VII, I shall have a little to say about these two latter subjects. In this one I want to consider State action in regard to production, the building up of real income. To this end, so as not to mix together different sets of influences, I shall provisionally ignore the fact that different people have incomes of different sizes. This fact will, of course, have to be brought into account later on, but not now.

Distributional considerations then being ignored, it is sometimes argued that, if competition acts freely, the 'invisible hand', of which Adam Smith spoke, will so contrive that the pursuit by each of his own private interest in the field of production will promote the aggregate interest of all. The argument runs like this. Under the sway of competition resources will be turned to producing different things in such a way that the last unit of resources devoted to any one thing satisfies a money demand equal to that satisfied by the last (that is the least wanted) unit devoted to any other thing. For, if this were not so, it would pay to shift units away from things that satisfy a smaller to things that satisfy a larger money demand. But, where people are equally rich, we may presume in a general way that a shilling means much the same for all of them, in technical language, that the marginal utility of money is the same for all of them. It follows — subject to a qualification about the relation between desires and satisfactions — that, if free competition causes resources to be so allocated that the least-wanted units in all of them satisfy equal money demands, they must also yield equal amounts of satisfaction. Any shifting of resources, therefore, away from the pattern in which free competition allocates them would entail the shifted units contributing a reduced yield of satisfaction. That is to say, any interference by the State with the arrangements that free competition tends to bring about would diminish the aggregate satisfaction enjoyed by, and so presumably the aggregate welfare of, the community as a whole. The argument which I have in this way roughly sketched out can, of course, easily be given an exact mathematical form. What is there to say about it ?

There are two main qualifications to be made. First, the argument tacitly assumes that to maximise satisfaction is equivalent to maximising welfare. But is that so ? Satisfactions have quality, not merely quantity; and bad kinds of satisfaction can hardly contribute to welfare, if welfare means, as presumably it must, something that is not merely desired but is also good. Obviously we are approaching very thin philosophical ice. I shall not go any nearer to that, but shall illustrate what I mean by a practical example. Some people keenly desire and get a great deal of satisfaction out of large and rapid consumption of alcohol or of opium. But other people, and on occasions these people themselves, think those satis-

factions bad, or, at all events, second-rate. On that ground
— or partly on that ground — governments make it difficult for people to buy opium and put taxes on alcoholic
drinks. A Chancellor of the Exchequer, in that part of
his Budget speech which deals with taxes on beer or
whisky, is always happy. If people have been drinking
more, the revenue from these duties is up, and he says,
" Splendid ". If people have been drinking less, so that
the revenue is down, the nation is becoming more sober
and he can still say, " Splendid ". What it all comes to,
then, is simply this. Even if free competition does maximise satisfaction, there may still be a case for some sorts
of State interference on ethical grounds.

This kind of consideration lies outside the economist's
proper field. But the second qualification we have to
discuss is entirely within that field. The gist of it is this.
When productive resources are employed in certain ways,
they yield, besides the output that is sold in the market,
a by-product, which may be beneficial or may be damag-
ing to people quite other than those who purchase the
main product, and for which nobody makes any payment.
The satisfaction or dissatisfaction which this by-product
carries does not, therefore, enter into the calculations of
the people who decide how much resources shall be
employed in making it. But, for aggregate satisfaction
to be maximised, it would have to enter into these calculations. So far as a particular use of resources yields
a by-product of unpaid-for satisfaction, too little resources
are turned into that use under the free play of competition.
So far as a particular use yields a by-product of unpenal-
ised dissatisfaction, too much resources are turned into it.
In either event there is a case for State intervention.

The point I have been making is easily illustrated.
Thus, when a factory emits a large amount of black smoke,
the damage done by that to the comfort of neighbours,
the addition made to their washing bill and so on, are

part of the cost entailed in the production of the factory's output. But the factory owners don't have to pay those costs. Therefore they devote to their output more resources than in the general interest they ought to do. Again, the sale of alcohol at public-houses entails an indirect cost in policemen. If the cost of the policemen were charged on the industry the scale of it would be cut down. Since the cost is not charged on it, it is too big. There are also cases of an opposite kind. Suppose somebody plants and maintains a forest in a dry district. Very likely the climate of the neighbourhood is improved and many people benefit; but the forest planter gets no payment for that. Again, somebody puts up a beautiful building — shall we say, or shall we not say, the University Library? No payment is made to him for the aesthetic pleasure this gives to the people who see it. Or again, consider such services as those rendered by light-houses or by campaigns for the destruction of locusts or malaria-carrying mosquitoes. It is impracticable for the people who undertake such enterprises to make individual charges for their services to those who benefit from them. Or again, take roads. It is not, indeed, altogether impracticable, but it is extraordinarily inconvenient, to finance the building and upkeep of these by levying tolls at turnpikes on the people who use them. The consequence is that, if we rely on the unassisted play of free competition for providing services of these sorts, much less resources will be devoted to providing them than it is in the general interest should be so devoted. Thus with this class of service there is a case for State intervention to secure that more is provided than would be provided if it stood aside; with the opposite class of service there is a case for its intervention to secure that less is provided.

There are a variety of forms which State action to these ends might take. It might leave the provision of both sorts of service to private enterprise, restricting the scope of some by taxes and expanding that of others by sub-sidies — subsidies, which, with such things as light-houses, would have to cover practically the whole of the cost. Alternatively, it might take over the provision of the two types of service itself, and so settle how much of them should be provided by direct fiat instead of indirectly by penalties and stimulants.

So far we have been thinking about conditions of free competition. When in any part of industry these con-ditions are violated and, instead of a large number of competing employers, we have one or a few individually big enough to exercise some degree of monopoly power, nobody has ever supposed that the self-interest of each tends to promote the aggregate welfare of all. A concern possessing monopoly power is able to force up prices so as to secure abnormal profits for itself. This entails, not merely a transfer of income to it, but also a reduction in the output of the goods and services it controls below the level at which they would be standing under competition, and so, subject to what I have just been saying, below the level that is best for aggregate economic welfare.

Now there are some kinds of services and goods which for technical reasons it is more economical to provide through a single agency than through a number of rival agencies. Obviously, for example, it would be extremely wasteful to have several different water companies, gas companies, electric power companies, telegraph companies or tramway companies laying down separate sets of pipes, or wires, or rails in the same district. It would be equally wasteful to have a number of rival railway companies covering the country with competing lines, all joining the same localities. In short, for all those services or goods that can only be distributed to purchasers through the agency of a complex network of equipment, common sense requires that this equipment shall not be needlessly duplicated but shall be held in a single hand. This entails that services providing water, gas, electricity, telephones, tramways and railways communication, cannot be run as competitive enterprises, but must in the main, in each several district, function as monopolies.

Now, everybody knows that, when something is being offered for sale by a number of competing producers, the purchasers are protected against exorbitant charges, yielding abnormally high returns to the seller, by the fact that, if one seller asks an exorbitant price, it will pay other sellers to undercut him. But when there is only one seller this protection is absent. A monopolist has the power to charge prices higher than are needed to yield him an ordinary rate of profit. He can levy a sort of tax on his customers for his own enrichment. Now the laying of pipes, wires, railway lines and so on, without which these monopolists cannot operate, requires some public action — perhaps the passage of a private Bill through Parliament. Because of this, apart from any other consideration, it is generally agreed that private persons, if they are allowed to lay them, must not be allowed, on the strength of that privilege, to mulct the public in unreasonable charges. So far there is agreement. But at this point divergence of view arises. Some persons would allow these services to be operated by private concerns, subject to conditions imposed on them by public authorities with the purpose of preventing them from charging excessive prices. Other persons would prefer that the public authorities should themselves operate concerns of this kind — that there should be municipal water supplies, gas supplies and tramways, and national, or possibly regional, railway systems and electricity systems.

Obviously this issue cannot be settled in categorical fashion. For there are a variety of different ways of controlling the concerns if they are in private hands and a variety of different ways of operating them if they are in public hands. It is thus not a question of comparing public control in a general way with public operation in a general way. A balance has to be struck, not once only, but on many occasions. It may well be that on different occasions it tips different ways. Moreover, the comparative advantages of control and operation may be different in given conditions for different types of concern : and different again for the same type of concern in countries with different traditions and different political organisations. Actual practical decisions, therefore, can only be made after a close study of the details of each case. All that one can do in a *general* discussion is to describe the principal types of public control on the one hand and of public operation on the other that have been widely practised or advocated.

Consider, first, methods by which the types of concern we are considering — so-called public utility concerns — can be controlled by public authorities while their actual operation is left in private hands. The purpose of the control is to prevent a concern, which necessarily possesses monopolistic power, from using that power to mulct the public and secure at their expense abnormal profits for its shareholders. Defence against this may be attempted by negative methods — laws against unreasonable charges, under which it is left to the courts to decide whether particular charges are in fact unreasonable — ; or by positive methods, under which maximum prices are specified for the goods and services produced. Under either plan the fundamental question, What prices are in fact reasonable ? has at some stage to be faced by somebody.

With public utility concerns the positive method is usually adopted. When this is done, since the relevant economic conditions are bound to alter from time to time, it is evident that any schedule of price maxima which is set up must be subject to revision at not over-long intervals. Sometimes an attempt is made to avoid the need for very frequent revisions by stipulating, not for absolute maximum prices, but for a sliding scale, under which the permitted maxima are tied to the rates of dividend that the public utility concerns are paying — tied to them in such a way that they are set lower, the higher the rate of dividend rises. This device has often been used in this country to regulate the charges made by gas companies. These sliding scales are, like sliding scales of wages, not substitutes for, but complements to, a system of periodic revision. If they were treated as permanent arrangements, all improvements and discoveries that reduced costs of production would steadily and continuously enhance profits. They are not easily organised for new companies, because the appropriate standards of price and dividend cannot be determined till some experience has been gained for the working of a concern. But it is feasible, and before the last war it was the practice of the Board of Trade, in dealing with gas companies, to fix a simple maximum price at first and to reserve power to substitute a sliding scale after the lapse of a certain interval.

Next consider ways in which public utility services, instead of being *controlled* by, can be *operated* by or on behalf of, public authorities. There are two principal ways. First, there is operation by a political authority, municipalities operating the town trams or gas supply through committees of the Town Council, the State operating the Post Office through a department of the Central Government. Secondly, there is operation by special *ad hoc* public boards deliberately divorced from direct political control — the Port of London Authority, the Electricity Commissioners, the British Broadcasting Corporation and so on.

Until comparatively recently the second of these methods was not used, and public operation meant, in effect, public operation by a public political authority already constituted for political purposes. Public operation of that type is open to attack by the advocates of private operation on three grounds. First, the political authorities, the Town Councils or the National Government, are organised with the view to their political duties ; and there is, therefore, no reason to suppose that they are well qualified to run economic enterprises. In particular, the methods of the Civil Service, appropriate enough for the normal business of Government, are not suitable for that quite different task ; nor are civil servants, whether attached to a Central Government or to local authorities, likely to possess the aptitudes and training required for it. Secondly, the area of these political authorities is settled with regard to what is appropriate politically and may not be well adapted to the economical running of tramways or electricity supply. The area covered by the Central Government might well be too large, that covered by municipal authorities too small. Thirdly, it is argued, particularly as against operation by the Central Government, that economic considerations in the running of these concerns would sometimes have to give way to a desire to catch votes.

The device of commissions or special *ad hoc* boards has been developed as a means of getting over these difficulties. Under it the controlling authorities are appointed by various groups of persons whose interests are affected. The Port of London Authority, for example, consists of representatives of payers of dues, wharfingers and owners of river craft, and of ten appointed members, of whom two must be representatives of Labour. The London Water Board consists of sixty-six members appointed by the local authorities of the area served. Authorities of this type are required to fix their charges in such a way as to cover interest on capital at a fixed rate, appropriate charges for depreciation and reserve, and, it may be, a contribution to the State. In some circumstances, in order to enable sufficient capital to be raised, it may be necessary for the State to guarantee interest upon it in case the Public Board's revenue should prove insufficient. When this is necessary and, may be, sometimes when it is not, the Boards are subjected in the last resort, not, of course, for purposes of normal administration, to the authority of a Minister of the State.

So far I have been speaking of undertakings that are in a position to exercise monopoly power because competitors cannot come in unless the public authorities intervene in their favour, giving them leave to lay pipes under the public streets, enabling them to buy land compulsorily (as with railway companies) and so on. But in a number of industries, where the most economical productive unit is very large or where rival employers get together in a price-fixing cartel, concerns which lie outside the public utility field may become possessed of strong monopoly power. The Rockefeller Oil Group and the United States Steel Corporation are outstanding examples of this ; while in this country also, in chemicals, iron and steel and a number of other industries, concerns exist that are in a similar position.

For cases of this kind the most stringent form of Government intervention by way of control is illustrated by the Sherman Anti-Trust Act passed many years ago in the United States. This Act sought to defend the public against monopolistic exactions by preventing combinations large enough to exercise monopoly power from being formed. The chief difficulty about this policy is that anti-trust laws are easily evaded. Particular forms of combination may be successfully banned, but other forms grow up, at the one end complete consolidations, at the other informal so-called gentlemen's agreements about prices. Also, if you stop combinations from being formed, you may sometimes compel an industry to organise itself in units of less than the most efficient size. A second method of control is an indirect one. The State does not try to prevent combinations from being formed and so maintain actual competition; but it penalises various devices, such as boycotts, discriminating price-cuts confined to selected regions and so on, by which a strong concern might frighten would-be competitors away. The idea is that, if newcomers are free to come in, existing concerns will be careful not to put prices too high for fear of tempting them to do so. In this way the public are indirectly defended in some degree. There are also, of course, available the negative and positive methods of price control that I spoke about in connection with public utility concerns. These methods are more difficult to apply effectively to concerns that make a great variety of products — iron and steel products, for example — than they are with such things as gas-works and tramway services, whose products are few in number. Perhaps for this reason, whereas, as I said a while back, with public utility concerns positive methods, the fixing of definite price maxima, are usually resorted to, control over the prices charged by large concerns in ordinary industry, when it is attempted at all, is more often worked by negative methods — penalties against unreasonable prices, with the decision as to what prices are in fact unreasonable left to the courts.

The alternative method of defence against monopoly, namely public operation, would also have to overcome greater technical difficulties in ordinary industries than in such things as municipal gas-works or even national railways, partly because the boundaries of the field to be covered would be more difficult to define. In Russia these difficulties have been overcome and the generality of large industries are in fact operated by public authorities. But hitherto in the Anglo-Saxon countries outside the public utility field public authorities have not gone beyond regulation and control.

So far, in discussing the rôle of Government in relation to production, we have left out of account the fact that different people have incomes of different sizes. By ignoring that fact, we have up to now been able to assume that, when two men are both willing to pay 1s. for something, that something will yield much the same amount of satisfaction to both of them. But, of course, in real life differences of income not only exist but are extensive and very important. To a man earning £3 a week 1s. means enormously more than it does to one earning £30 a week. If the poorer man is willing to spend 1s. on something, it is pretty certain that he expects from it an amount of satisfaction equal to what the rich man expects from spending, not one, but a great many shillings. This destroys the presumption that, by spreading productive resources among different things in such a way that the demand prices offered for the last unit engaged on any one thing is equal to that offered for the last unit engaged on any other, we shall maximise aggregate satisfaction. Plainly satisfaction would be increased if some of the resources devoted to making mink coats and champagne for the rich could be diverted to making ordinary clothes and beer for the poor; provided that this could be done without serious damage to aggregate production. Plainly, too, subject to that proviso, aggregate satisfaction would be much increased if some part of the income of the rich could be transferred to the poor. It follows that the conclusions we have reached may be upset in cases where what is good for production is bad for distribution, or *vice versa*. In such cases conflicting tendencies are at work and a balance has somehow to be struck between them.

CHAPTER VI

THE PROPORTION OF INCOME-GETTING POWER AT WORK ON THE AVERAGE AND AT DIFFERENT TIMES

IN the second chapter I discussed the various influences by which the scale of a country's income-getting power is determined. This, as we have seen, depends at any time on the amount and quality of its land, the number and quality of its people and the quantity and character of its capital equipment and organisation. It changes with changes in these things, and also with developments in scientific knowledge and industrial skill. It depends, too, as was shown in the third chapter, on its dealings with other countries ; though, for the present argument, I shall for the most part leave that out of account. Now to know what a country's income-getting power is is to know in principle what amount of real income of given pattern it could produce if the whole of that income-getting power were fully employed. But in fact over the average of a long period there is always a significant proportion of it not employed. Moreover, from time to time the proportion that is not employed is found by experience to fluctuate substantially above and below the average. Thus even complete knowledge about how a country's income-getting power is determined would give us a far from complete knowledge about how its real income is determined. For that we need to know also how the average proportion of this power which is actually at work is determined and how variations in actual proportions about the average are determined. In this chapter I shall begin with a short account of the facts, so far as they are known for this country, and then shall try in a very rough way to describe the chief influences by which they are brought about. On this subject there are still considerable differences of opinion among economists — much more than there are about those discussed in earlier chapters.

Income-getting power consists, as I have said, of a number of different elements. But there is only one of them about whose activity there are good statistics. That is labour power. The activity of this and that of industrial equipment presumably vary more or less together. We may, therefore, reasonably use the percentages of would-be wage-earners who are actually employed as a rough indication of the extent to which the country's income-getting power is being exercised. For Great Britain certain trade unions have published returns about employment over a long period, and, since the 1914–18 war, there have been available more broadly-based figures collected in connection with unemployment insurance. These two sets of statistics are not exactly comparable. But, making rough adjustments, we may say that, on the average of the half-century before 1914, of the available labour about 6 per cent was unemployed, and on the average of the inter-war period about 14 per cent. The earlier of these two periods was characterised by a number of successive wave movements, nearly all of them lasting not less than five or more than ten years ; the average unemployment percentage in each of them being not far off the average for all of them together. The second period, 1921–38, was not long enough to show such clear-cut tendencies. But employment improved up to 1924, worsened substantially from 1929 to 1932, and then improved again till shortly before the outbreak of the recent war. In both periods employment varied somewhat between different seasons of the year. But the annual variations were much larger and more important. In the earlier period the maximum annual percentage of unemployment exceeded the average percentage by 7 and the minimum figure fell below the average by $2\frac{1}{2}$. In the second period the excess of the maximum over the average percentage was 8 and the deficiency of the minimum below the average was $4\frac{1}{2}$. We may thus say broadly that the average percentage of unemployment in the second period was some $2\frac{1}{2}$ times as large as in the first ; but the absolute range of deviations about the average was not markedly different in the two periods. You will notice, of course, that these percentages are percentages of *unemployment*. The average percentages of available workers *employed* were in the two periods 94 and 86. Thus the broad difference between the two periods was that on the average of the second, $\frac{8}{10}$ths, on the average of the first, $\frac{7}{10}$ths of the available labour force was actually engaged in work. This is, of course, only another way of saying what I have already said in terms of *un*employment. But it puts the fact in better perspective. It makes it clear that the difference between the two periods was much less catastrophic than a comparison of the unemployment figures by themselves might at first sight suggest. After all, on the average of the second as well as on that of the first period, by far the predominant part of the available labour force was not idle against its will but was exercising its income-producing power.

So much for the facts. We have now to try to explain them. First, why was the average level of unemployment so much higher in the inter-war period than it had been before 1914 ? That it really was much higher — that we are not merely being tricked into thinking it was higher because the figures were collected on a different basis — nobody seriously doubts. But as to why it was higher there is a great deal of uncertainty.

The severe dislocations due to the war and its aftermath must clearly have had something to do with it. Many fewer people came to be needed in the export industries, in coal-mining and in shipbuilding, than were needed there before the war. During the war itself, in ship-building and in munition industries the number of work-people assembled was much greater than before the war, and the excess after the war over the numbers needed was correspondingly larger. Under the influence of the changed conditions of demand when the war stopped, men tended, of course, to move out of the overcrowded industries. But the adjustment was in some cases very slow. It was very difficult for coal-miners to leave their villages and seek work elsewhere ; they stayed on in the hope that demand for the kind of work in which they were skilled would soon revive. Moreover, unemployment was so widespread that, unless their moving into new industries caused wages there to fall and so created a new demand, it might well involve merely a redistribution of unemployment among places and occupations without appreciably reducing the volume of unemployment as a whole. It is impossible to say how large a part these war-time and post-war dislocations in particular industries played in bringing about the excess aggregate unemploy-ment of the inter-war years. Very few economists, if any, would attribute the whole, or nearly the whole, of the excess to them. They look rather, or at all events, also, to some more fundamental maladjustment between aggre-gate money outlay, which constitutes the effective demand for goods and services, and the mean rate of money wages.

About the nature and origins of this maladjustment there are wide differences of opinion. Here is a tentative suggestion for what it is worth. Wage-earners are always pressing for higher rates of wages and employers are always resisting the pressure. But the pressure is relatively strong when employment is good and relatively weak when it is bad. The reason is that, when employment is bad, trade unions are especially reluctant to do anything that threatens to make it worse, partly because of the heavy drain that large unemployment puts on their funds and partly because of the direct suffering that it causes. In given psychological conditions and with given arrangements for looking after the unemployed the pressure on wages tends, I suggest, to be so regulated that the average percentage of unemployment over good and bad times together works out at some definite value. This is not merely an idle speculation. The trade union unemployment figures for the sixty years before the last war show eight waves or cycles of rising and falling employment. In no one of these was the average percentage of unemployment significantly less than 4 per cent or more than 6 per cent. This means, of course, that the average percentage of employment among people seeking work was not in any cycle more than 96 per cent or less than 94 per cent. This high degree of constancy was maintained in the face of a very large change in the number of would-be wage-earners seeking work. Between the 1881 and 1911 censuses the number of males recorded as gainfully occupied in Great Britain increased by no less than 45 per cent. The number of would-be wage-earners must, therefore, have increased roughly in that proportion. It is a striking fact that the average percentage of persons actually employed in the successive cycles should have remained very nearly constant in the face of so large a change.

But what bearing has this on the question why unemployment was so much heavier in the inter-war period than it was before 1914? It has this bearing. Soon after the last war the system of compulsory State-aided insurance against unemployment, which had been started on a small scale in 1911, was extended to cover practically the whole of industry. As a result of this the twofold restraint which had held back trade unions in pressing for increases and resisting decreases in wage rates was very greatly weakened. For now, if, by doing this, they indirectly make unemployment higher, the burden on their own finances and the suffering of the unemployed men will both be very much less than they used to be. This fact is bound to modify their wage policy to an important extent ; and to modify it in a way likely to make the unemployment percentage larger. There are no means of determining by objective tests how much of the extra unemployment that prevailed in the inter-war years was due to this cause. My own impression, or, if you prefer it, guess, is that a substantial part of it can be accounted for in this way.

Now pass away from the average level of employment or unemployment over the good and bad times of successive trade cycles, and consider fluctuations about the average. These, as I said, do not show markedly different characteristics in the period before 1914 and in the inter-war period. They may, therefore, be considered in a general way so as to cover both of them. A chart setting out the trade union percentages of unemployment from 1850 to 1914 would show a series of very marked wave-like fluctuations. Why did these fluctuations take place ? Why didn't the percentage of unemployment, and so the percentage of employment, continue at round about the same level all the time? What generates the waves and what influences govern their size? In a discussion like this I can't possibly explore these very large questions; I can only set up landmarks and call attention to salient points.

There is and has long been fairly general agreement among economists that the immediate cause lying behind general fluctuations of employment consists in changes in the expectations of business men about future prospects, or, to use a looser term, in business confidence. There is also general agreement that these changes in expectations show themselves predominantly in swings in the demand for labour for investment — chiefly for investment in works of construction. Thus a main feature of the boom which culminated in 1825 was investment in Mexican mines and other enterprises in the South American countries recently freed from Spain. In 1833–6 there was large investment in railway building in England and in the United States. The crisis of 1847 was associated with a tremendous boom in English railway building. Before the 1857 crisis we had made large investments in, and had exported much material for, American railways. In the early 'sixties there was another British railway boom and in the early 'seventies another American one. The Baring crisis followed large investments in railways in Argentina. The beginning of the twentieth century witnessed a great expansion of electrical enterprise, especially in Germany, and the 1907 crisis, which started in the United States, followed upon a similar development there. Industrial expansions have always been, in the main, expansions in the building of means of production. What means of production are selected depends upon circumstances. As one writer puts it : " At the beginning of the nineteenth century it was the means for sewing and spinning — in a word, all kinds of textile machinery ; — a little later it was a formidable apparatus of railways and railway material and of steamships to take the place of wooden sailing vessels ; in our own day — this was written thirty years ago — it is electrical energy and its manifold industrial applications, tramways, electric railways, electric furnaces, electric light and so on " [1]

So much, as I have said, is pretty generally agreed. But why do the variations in business expectations that take place and that show themselves in these forms occur at all ? Some writers find an explanation in the fact that technical advances, opening up new profitable fields for investment, are made, not smoothly and continuously, but by jumps. Thus one authority writes : " The history

[1] Lescure, *Les Crises générales et périodiques*, 2nd edition, p. 412.

of cycles and crises teaches us that the jumpy increases of investment characterising every boom are usually connected with some definite technical advance. In fact the beginnings of almost every modern technical achievement — the railway, the iron and steel industry, the electrical industry, the chemical industry and, most recently, the automobile industry — can be traced back to a boom. It seems as if our economic system reacts to the stimulus of some technical advance with the prompt and complete mobilisation of all its inner forces in order to carry it out in the shortest possible time." [1] But there is a serious difficulty in the way of this explanation. No doubt, industrial activity expands when technical advances are being *exploited*. But this doesn't allow us to say that the expansions are *caused* by technical advances — discoveries and inventions — unless these advances are exploited at the time when they are made. In fact there is usually a very considerable lag between discovery or invention and its exploitation. This is well illustrated by the history of railway development in this country. The Stockton and Darlington Railway was opened in 1825 and Huskisson was killed by the Rocket in 1830; but the most important railway boom did not develop till 1845. We cannot, therefore, explain that boom merely by reference to Stephenson's invention of the steam locomotive. What seems to happen is that in slack periods technical devices and improvements often accumulate in the sphere of knowledge, but are not exploited until times improve. So far as this is so, it looks as though they rather provide the channels into which activity will flow when it is ripe to expand than themselves directly cause the expansions.

An alternative explanation dating back to Stanley Jevons, eighty years ago, looks to variations in the yield of crops in agricultural countries. When these countries

---

[1] Röpke, *Crises and Cycles*, p. 98.

enjoy specially good crops, people there can afford to buy more manufacturing goods and machinery from industrial countries. This gives a fillip to activity there. Conversely, when crops in the agricultural countries are bad, their people cannot afford to buy so much abroad, and this has a depressing influence on the industrial countries. But there are difficulties about this type of explanation, which seriously limit its scope. I do not want to go into them. For, though it may well be that some improvements and worsenings in business men's views about industrial prospects are due to them, nobody would seriously argue that they can account for anything like all of these.

Rather, it is fairly obvious that the expectations which guide the action of the persons in control of industry are liable to be influenced favourably or unfavourably, not by one single sort of cause only, but by a number of different causes. A serious industrial dispute may affect them a great deal; the erection of a high tariff or the abolition of a high tariff in an important foreign country; a monetary change abroad; political disturbances; wars and rumours of wars; peace and rumours of peace — any of these, when psychological conditions are suitable, may touch off the spark, and, as the case may be, set going an upward or a downward movement in industrial activity and employment.

But the question by what impulses upward and downward waves of activity are started is of less interest than the question by what processes these wave movements, when they are started, develop. Here psychological influences — mutual infection towards excessive optimism and excessive pessimism — certainly play a considerable part, just as they do in our predictions about how and when a war is going to end. But there is also a process more definite than this, which has been described in a very interesting way by Professor Schumpeter. This is what he writes: "Only a few people possess the quality of leadership — the quality of actually introducing and under-taking new combinations — which is quite a different thing from inventing them. However, if one or a few have advanced with success, many of the difficulties disappear. Others can then follow these pioneers, as they will clearly do under the stimulus of the success now obtainable. Their success again makes it easier . . . for more people to follow suit, until finally the innovation becomes familiar and the acceptance of it a matter of free choice. . . . The successful appearance of an entrepreneur (one who carries out new combinations) is followed by the appear-ance, not simply of some others, but of ever greater numbers, though progressively less qualified. . . . Every normal boom starts in one or a few branches of industry and . . . derives its character from the innovations in the industry where it begins. But the pioneers remove the obstacles for the others, not only in the branch of production in which they first appear, but, owing to the nature of these obstacles, *ipso facto* in other branches too." [1]

The question, by what processes upward and downward movements in business men's expectations, and so in industrial activity, develop, runs into another and very closely related question ; by what influences are the amplitude, or width of range, of the fluctuations to which the processes lead determined ? There are, of course, a number of influences. I shall not try to list them. But look at one, which certainly plays a very important part : monetary arrangements or, perhaps better, monetary arrangements and wage arrangements taken together. When business men think prospects good they finance increased activity partly by turning over their balances more frequently than usual and partly by borrowing money from the banks. In consequence of this, money income expands, and, as experience shows, it usually expands

[1] Schumpeter, *The Theory of Economic Development*, pp. 228-9.

faster than real income — the output of goods and ser- vices. Therefore, since money income is expended on buying real income, the general level of prices, including the prices of consumption goods, goes up. This causes wage-earners to ask for higher rates of money wages. But there is always a lag about this movement. Conse- quently, for a time employers find that the prices of the goods they make have risen more than in proportion to the wages they have to pay; so that they get a special profit. So long as this state of things lasts, they are stimulated to engage more work-people; the initial bettering in their expectations sets up causes which justify a still further improvement; and so on. There are a number of different ways in which these happenings can be described. But the dominant factor governing the amplitude of upward fluctuations in employment — and obviously the same thing is true of downward fluctuations — is the degree of freedom with which money income is able to expand or contract. This depends largely on the policy of the Government about currency and of the banks about loans. It is always possible to prevent money income from rising more than is desired by putting rates of discount high enough and drawing off money from circulation by the sale of securities against money on the part of the banks. Therefore, though, as I shall show in a moment, it is *not* always possible to prevent money income from *falling* more than is desired by operations of an opposite kind, the amplitude of industrial and employment fluctuations depends to an important extent on the kind of monetary and banking policy that is being followed.

There is, of course, a great deal more that might be said about these and allied matters. But at the present time people are much more interested in practical schemes for improving the employment situation than in the diagnosis of causes — what steps can or should the State or other authorities take in this field ? I therefore pass to that problem. In doing this I shall reverse the order with which I started, and, for a reason that will become clear presently, shall speak first about fluctuations in, not about the average level of, employment.

At one time it was widely held, and is still held by at least one economist of authority, that money outlay — or, more strictly, money outlay per head — could be effectively stabilised and, therefore, fluctuations in employment almost completely abolished by a sufficiently skilful handling of monetary and banking machinery. But most economists are now agreed that conditions may easily occur where this will not be enough. As I have said, to stop upward fluctuations should always be technically possible — though this does not, of course, imply that it is always politically possible. But in the face of downward fluctuations monetary and banking remedies may easily break down. For this there are two reasons. First, whereas there is no limit to the extent to which the banking system, if it chooses, can force the rate of discount up, there is a limit below which it cannot force it down. Whatever might be conceivable in theory, in practice you cannot have negative rates of discount. But, in order to stop declines in money income, you might, in a deep depression, need negative rates. Secondly, whereas in times of boom the banks, by selling securities, can drag money out of circulation and, by that route, force money income down, in times of depression corresponding action is not always open to them. True, they can buy securities from the public and so increase as much as they choose the quantity of money in people's balances. But they can't compel people to use these balances. If prospects are bleak, there is nothing to prevent them from leaving them completely idle as savings deposits. If they do this, the money pumped into balances is not pumped into the *circulation*, and so does nothing to prevent money

INCOME

income from contracting below what is desired. Broadly,
then, whereas monetary and banking policy can always,
at least in principle, be relied on to stop booms, it cannot
always be relied on to prevent depressions.

For this reason attention has lately been focussed on
a different type of remedy for general fluctuations in
industrial activity and employment — a type of remedy
that is sometimes supposed to be a quite recent invention,
but was in fact canvassed, so far as its essential elements
go, between thirty and forty years ago in the Majority
and Minority reports of the Royal Commission on the
Poor Laws.   The general idea is extremely simple.
Experience shows that the demand for labour on the part
of private industry moves up and down as business men's
expectations of profit vary.   Why should not public
authorities, who are not controlled by the profit motive,
arrange their demand in such a way as to offset fluctuations in private demand and so make demand as a whole,
and, consequently, the sum-total of employment, much
more stable than it is ?   Obviously there are large and
important parts of public demand that cannot be switched
about at will in the interest of stability.   When a new
school is urgently needed in some district or a new battle-
ship to replace one that has been lost, these things must
be provided there and then ; orders for them cannot be
postponed so as to dovetail into periods of industrial
depression.   But there is a good deal of normal public
expenditure that *can* be switched about.   There is nothing
to prevent programmes being prepared of work that is
useful but not urgent, the main part of them to be carried
out when private industry is slack rather than when it
is active.   In the White Paper on Employment Policy
published in May 1944 considerable stress is laid on this.
Here is the relevant passage : " The Government believe
that in the past the power of public expenditure, skilfully
applied, to check the onset of a depression has been under-

96

estimated. The whole notion of pressing forward quickly with public expenditure when incomes were falling and the outlook was dark has, naturally enough, encountered strong resistance from persons who are accustomed, with good reason, to conduct their private affairs according to the very opposite principle. Such resistance can, however, be overcome if public opinion is brought to the view that periods of trade recession provide an opportunity to improve the permanent equipment of society by the provision of better housing, public buildings, means of communication, power and water supplies, etc."[1]

I said a little while back that I would speak about remedies for fluctuations in employment before remedies for high average unemployment for a reason that would appear presently. The reason is that the most discussed remedy for fluctuations, the one I have just been describing, is also, in its degree, a remedy for high average unemployment. Of course, to lessen fluctuations is, as a matter of mere arithmetic, quite compatible with leaving average unemployment untouched. Average unemployment is exactly the same whether the annual figure stands constant at $7\frac{1}{2}$ per cent or oscillates between 5 and 10 per cent. But the particular policy aimed at lessening fluctuations which I have been describing does in fact affect the average level of unemployment also. It affects it in two ways.

First, when general demand is fluctuating there are sure to be a number of centres and occupations in which in good times part of the demand fails to realise itself in employment, going to waste, so to speak, in vacancies that employers would like, but are not able, to fill. Consequently, when demand is stabilised, so that such-and-such a decrease of demand in good times is combined with an equal increase in bad times, the reduction of employment in good times is less than the reduction in demand, but the increase of employment in bad times is equal to the increase in demand. This means that the *average* level of employment is raised.

Secondly, when there is an upward fluctuation in demand, there is no ceiling to put a stop to the upward movement in wage rates that is likely to be associated with it. But, when there is a downward fluctuation, there is a very definite bottom below which wage rates cannot in any event fall. This is established partly by public sentiment about what constitutes a reasonable wage and partly by the fact that people can reckon to receive certain minimum sums from the unemployment fund, even if they are doing no work at all. This asymmetry between the effects on wage rates of upward and downward movements of demand entails that to stabilise demand at the average of what it used to be carries with it a lowering in the average rate of wages over good and bad times together, and so probably makes it worth while for employers to engage more men. There is a certain amount of controversy about this. But, in my opinion, policies of stabilising demand for labour are likely for these two reasons, not merely to lessen the extent to which employment fluctuates, but also appreciably to raise the average level of it over good and bad times taken together.

This stabilisation policy is one of the principal proposals in the Government White Paper. It is becoming fashionable in some quarters to throw cold water upon it on the ground that, even if it were fully carried out, a good deal of preventable unemployment — unemployment, that is, over and above the inevitable minimum which must arise from people changing over from one firm or one job to another — would still be left. It is suggested that public authorities ought to try, not merely to stabilise aggregate demand, but to raise the average level of it by pressing forward continuously with a long-term programme of planned outlay directed, to quote Sir William

Beveridge, " against the giant social evils of want, disease, squalor and ignorance and towards the raising of productivity by improvements of our capital equipment ".[1] There is a great deal to be said for such a programme for its own sake, apart altogether from any effect that it may have on employment. But, so far as its effect on that go, we should do well to be on guard against exaggerated hopes. If, as experience shows to be likely, upward tendencies in the demand for labour call into play associated upward tendencies in money rates of wages, the benefit to employment might well turn out to be a good deal less than was expected. Wage-earners might, in effect, choose better money wage rates *instead of* better employment. Up to a point they might enjoy something of both. But beyond a point it is impossible for them to get both except at the risk of bringing into play a spiral of monetary inflation so rapid as to threaten serious social evils. Obviously I cannot go into that complicated matter ; nor yet consider here the bearing of war-time experience upon the consequences that are likely to result from rapid monetary inflation in times of peace.

[1] Beveridge, *Full Employment in a Free Society*, p. 272.

CHAPTER VII

THE DISTRIBUTION OF INCOME AMONG PEOPLE

THE subject of this chapter is the distribution of income among people. For this discussion it is convenient to give the term income a rather different meaning from what it had when we were thinking about net national income. That included income from Government property as well as private income, and excluded transfer payments — of which the most important are national debt interest, pensions, unemployment benefit and so on. The income we are now interested in is what the Chancellor of the Exchequer's White Paper calls " Private Income ", so defined as to exclude income from Government property and to include these transfer payments. For this country in 1938 income from Government property amounted to only £44 millions, as against the total of private income of over £5000 millions. We need not, therefore, bother about it. But transfer payments amounted to £478 millions, nearly 10 per cent of private income. The fact, therefore, that for the present purpose we are going to count these as income must not be forgotten. A certain awkwardness is involved, too, because, with this use of words, when money is collected from one set of people in taxes and handed over to another set, say in the form of gratuitous pensions, new income is created to the extent of the pensions. Though, therefore, we may say that purchasing power is transferred, we should not in strictness say that income is transferred. This, however, is a difficulty about the use of words, not about things. According to the White Paper, private income — that is, of course, private income before tax — amounted in 1938 to £5038 millions, nineteen-twentieths of which was what the Chancellor called "personal income", and one-twentieth "impersonal income" in the form of undistributed profits of companies, the expenditure of which the shareholders, to whom, of course, it belonged, did not individually control. This figure of approximately £5000 millions for 1938 is a useful one to remember. The corresponding figure given in the White Paper for 1943 was £8700 millions. But for my present purpose it is convenient to take such statistics as we need from the last full pre-war year and not to bring into account the abnormal conditions of war-time.

So much for the meaning of our principal term. Now for the problem. If for a community of adult men of the same race we were to draw up a table giving the number of people of all different heights, five foot one inch, five foot six, six feet and so on, and set out these numbers on a chart, marking off height on the x axis and numbers at the several heights on the y axis, we should get a graph more or less like a cocked hat, technically known as the normal curve of error. The most frequent height would be the average height and, as you moved away from that in either direction, you would get fewer and fewer people at each successive height. The numbers would be grouped symmetrically about the mean, the same number at 3 inches above it as at 3 inches below it, and so on. The same sort of distribution would be found for weights and, on some tests, for intelligence. As you probably know, in large-scale examinations a check-up is sometimes made on the reliability of particular examiners by seeing whether the distribution of their marks approximates to a normal curve. This sort of distribution is to be expected when the differences among individual magnitudes that are being measured result from the interplay of a large number of independent causes whose individual effects are small. All this is well known. The point I want to make is that the distribution of income among people in this or any other Western country, if plotted out on a chart, would *not* resemble the normal curve of error. Whereas, as I have said, with heights and so on, the number of people below the average is about the same as the number above it, very tall people being about as numerous as very short and moderately tall as moderately short, with incomes the number below the average is much greater than the number above it. There are a comparatively small number of giants, whose presence raises the average height above the height to which the great bulk of the people attain. Thus the distribution of income among people is different in character from what at the first approach a student, say, of biology might expect to find

Some of the facts about income distribution in this country in 1938 are brought together in the Chancellor of the Exchequer's 1944 White Paper, to which I have referred. Of private incomes at the disposal of individuals (excluding undistributed profits and including transfer incomes) something like 4 per cent accrued to 8000 income-receivers with more than £10,000 a year each, that is to say, on the assumption that each of these income-receivers maintains four persons, to about one-tenth of 1 per cent of the population; something like 12 per cent to 105,000 income-receivers with more than £2000 a year, representing some 1 per cent of the population; one-quarter to 800,000 income-receivers with more than £500 a year, representing 7 per cent of the population. There was thus obviously a very strong concentration of income towards the upper end of the scale.

Various writers, particularly Mr. Colin Clark, have tried to carry this statistical analysis of distribution into closer detail. But Dr. Bowley, who is the leading authority on these matters, is very sceptical about such attempts. He even writes: " There is nothing to be gained by endeavouring to classify incomes below £2000 according to their amount and a good deal to be lost by publishing with spurious accuracy statistics based largely on guess-work ".[1] Still he allows that the estimates offered by Sir John Orr in his book, *Food, Health and Income*, published in 1936, " are probably broadly correct ".[2] These — they are worked out for 1934 — suggest that about three-tenths of the population, and one-half of the children under fourteen in this country, were living in families in which weekly income per head was less than 15s. ; and seven-tenths of the population, and five-sixths of the children in families in which it was less than 30s. Alongside these figures he put estimates, first of the minimum income per head that would provide adequate nutrition if expenditure was arranged in the best possible way, and secondly, of the minimum needed for this with expenditure arranged more or less as it actually is. The first — his ' theoretical ' minimum — for proper nutrition he put at 14s. 6d., the second, his ' reasonable ' minimum, at 25s. per head. This suggests that in 1934 nearly half the children of the country lived in families where it was impossible for the family income to provide them with enough food, and more than three-quarters in families where it was unlikely that it would provide enough. These very small incomes of the many stand in sharp and challenging contrast with the very large incomes enjoyed by a fortunate few.

What are the influences upon which the distribution of income among persons, with this high concentration upon a comparatively small number at the top end of the scale, chiefly depend ? People receive incomes in the main as payment for services rendered by their own work of brain and hand and by productive equipment owned by them. With the definition of income we are here using we have to add that some income is received in the form of transfers to which the recipients have contractual

[1] *Studies in National Income*, p. 118.   [2] *Ibid.*

or other legal rights — national debt interest, pensions and so on. But, as we have seen, this part, though it must not be forgotten, only amounts to some 10 per cent of the whole and need not disturb the argument. It is easy to see, then, that the way in which income is dis= tributed among persons depends *immediately* upon two sets of facts : first, the rates of pay which various sorts of productive power, Labour power, Capital, Land and their subdivisions, are earning per unit ; and, secondly, upon the way in which the ownership of these various sorts of productive power are distributed among persons. *Ulti- mately*, therefore, it depends, first upon the influences which determine the rates of pay of various productive agents, and secondly upon those which determine the distribution among people of the ownership of these agents. The discussion of the first of these two sets of influences — those determining the distribution of income among factors of production, as the usual phrasing goes — has long constituted an important part of economics. The second set lies on the border-line between economics and general sociology. I shall have something to say about both.

Let us begin with the first. So that the main features of the problem may stand out clearly, I shall make rather a drastic simplification. I shall ignore the fact that in actual life a great number of different sorts of goods and services are produced and sold ; and shall imagine that there is only one single sort, for example wheat. With this model it is natural to discuss distribution in terms of this single thing, wheat, and there is no point in bringing in money. An outline picture of what happens can be sketched out like this : All the various productive agents, labour of various kinds, capital instruments of various kinds, land of various kinds, co-operate together to yield the total net income of wheat that is produced every year. Since, then, each unit of every agent of production is helped in its work by all the others, as workmen, for example, are helped by their tools, the more of any agent there is, when the quantities of the others are given, the less difference to total output will be made by taking on an additional unit, or by dispensing with a unit, of that agent. For, with a thousand units already at work, a new unit will get less help from the other agents than it would do if only a hundred units were at work. If, with a given stock of capital and land, labour is very abundant, the difference made to total output by adding one more workman will be much smaller than if labour is very scarce. The same thing is true of machines and of pieces of land. All this may be expressed by saying that, when the quantity of the other agents of production are given, additions to the quantity of any one agent yield diminishing returns of output. But, since the several agents are hired out by controllers of industry, who look to make a profit by hiring them, the rates of pay in wheat per unit offered to each of them will approximate, under conditions of competition, to the difference which is made to output by adding or subtracting a single unit. It follows that, given the quantity of the other agents of production, the rate of pay in wheat per unit of any one agent will be smaller the more abundant that agent is.

When we abandon the assumption that only one sort of thing is being produced, the analysis is, of course, much more complicated. Account, for example, will have to be taken of the practice in some industries of monopolistic restrictions ; and there are a variety of other awkwardnesses. Still the broad result remains the same. Other things being equal, the more of any agent of production there is, the smaller the rate of pay per unit that it is likely to get. The more coal-miners there are, the more doctors, the more schoolmasters, the less in given conditions will be their rates of pay ; the more capital there is, the lower the rate of interest it will be able to command ; the more land there is, relatively to labour and capital equipment, the lower the rent per acre. Everywhere relative abundance means low pay per unit, relative scarcity high pay per unit.

You will have noticed that I have been careful to speak throughout of rates of pay *per unit*. The fact that, the more of any agent of production there is, the less, other things being equal, it will earn per unit does not imply that it will earn less in the aggregate. If you double the number of doctors, the average doctor will earn less, but doctors as a body, when account is taken of their increased numbers, may earn more. Whether they will in fact earn more or less depends on the character of the demand for their services ; whether it is such that a given increase in numbers causes the rate of pay per unit to fall off more or less than in proportion. If we divide the agents of production into three broad groups in the manner of the classical economists, we may, I think, take it as fairly certain that an increase in the quantity of any one of them will cause its rate of pay to fall less than proportionately ; so that its aggregate earnings will be increased. This is an important point. Suppose that, on account, say, of improved education, all wage-earners become twice as efficient, come to contain, so to speak, two units of work each instead of one. Unless the aggregate earnings of all the units of labour together are increased by the change, the representative workman, though producing more units of work every day, will find himself with a less daily wage than before. It is fortunate that the conditions which would lead to this paradoxical result are not likely to be realised in fact.

There is another point which is also important. Though the knowledge that an increase in the quantity of an agent of production will reduce its rate of pay per unit does not by itself tell us what will happen to the aggregate earnings of that agent, it does tell us what will happen to those of the other agents collectively. Suppose there were originally a thousand units of some agent, and the number is increased to eleven hundred. Total product is expanded. The original thousand units will get less of it than they used to get. The extra units do not get more than they add to total product. It follows that the aggregate earnings of the other agents of production collectively are increased by at least the cut in the rate of pay per unit of the expanded agent multiplied by a thousand. The same thing is almost certainly true of other agents individually, if we conceive individual agents broadly in the classical manner. Thus an increase in the volume of capital, even though this means that capital in the aggregate earns more, is almost certainly, not as is sometimes supposed, injurious to labour, but beneficial to it. The addition to its aggregate real earnings which capital gets is smaller than the accompanying addition to total product. Something is, therefore, left over to help out the earnings of labour.

What I have been saying must not be regarded as an account, even in barest outline, of the way in which the distribution of income among agents of production is determined. It is only an account of this on the assumption that the quantities of the several agents are fixed independently of the rates of pay that they are receiving But, of course, they are not so fixed. This means that influences on the side of supply as well as influences on the side of demand have a part to play. A mathematical set-up of the equations required to determine the several unknowns can be constructed without difficulty. But to cover the dry bones of that skeleton with flesh and blood is a very different thing. Great difficulties are involved, particularly difficulties connected with the element of time. It takes a very long while for reactions on supply — on the number of people trained for particular jobs, still more on the number of people born and growing up to working age — fully to work themselves out ; and, while that is happening, demand conditions themselves are sure to change. It would be quite beyond the scope of this book to go into all that. For the present purpose these few hints will have to serve.

Turn, then, to the second chief aspect of our problem. Suppose that the influences by which the rates of pay per unit of various sorts of productive agents are determined have been sufficiently described. The distribution of income among people depends then upon the way in which the ownership of these various income-getting agents is distributed among them. How is this in fact distributed and what are the influences by which the distribution is settled ? These income-getting agents fall into two main divisions : income-yielding property belonging to individual men and women, and the personal capacity for earning income embodied in these men and women themselves. Let us consider first the ownership of property.

In Mr. Campion's authoritative book, *Public and Private Property*, published in 1939, it is estimated that in 1936 " one per cent of the persons aged twenty-five and over in England and Wales owned 55 per cent of the total property in private hands " ; while, at the other extreme, three-quarters of these persons owned " only a little more than 5 per cent of the total property in private hands ".[1] Of course when it is said that one per cent of persons over twenty-five own over 55 per cent of the total property in private hands, this does not mean that only one per cent *benefit* from that proportion of it. If each of these persons was one of a married pair, the other of whom had no property, the percentage of persons over twenty-five *enjoying* 55 per cent of the total property would be, not one but two per cent. But it is not necessary to go into refinements. The crude figures amply show, on the one hand, that an enormous proportion of the country's privately

[1] *Loc. cit.* pp. 109-10.

THE DISTRIBUTION OF INCOME AMONG PEOPLE

owned property is concentrated among a very small number of persons, and, on the other hand, that a very large part of the population own per head an extremely small amount of property. Now if, with Mr. Campion, we put the proportion of private income, as here defined, that is derived from property at one-quarter,[1] the fact that (for 1936) from one to two per cent of persons over twenty-five owned 55 per cent of the privately owned property implies that this very small percentage of persons, by reason of their property rights alone, absorbed not much less than one-seventh (14 per cent) of the total money income. When this figure is taken in conjunction with the White Paper figure quoted earlier, which gave the richest one per cent of income-receivers for 1938 12 per cent of privately-owned income, it becomes evident that the high concentration of incomes upon the fortunate few is in large part immediately due to the way in which property is distributed. What are the influences that regulate that and promote this high degree of concentration ?

Private fortunes are achieved in two ways, by saving and by inheritance. This means that cumulative forces are at work. Large incomes make large savings possible; the capital acquired through these savings makes the saver's income still larger in the future, so that he can save at a still higher rate. In the same way the inheritance of a large fortune carries with it a large income, which enables savings to be made, so that the inherited fortune can be increased. These cumulative processes are bound to promote concentration in the ownership of property. To him that hath shall be given.

This is not all. A dominating influence is exerted by the policy which the State pursues as regards inheritance. There are substantial differences in the laws about this in different countries. The most important thing for our

---

[1] *Ibid.* p. 116.

present purpose is what the State does by way of absorbing the property of private persons when they die through death duties. Obviously a system of steeply graduated duties rising to very high rates at the upper end must greatly reduce the range of inequality among fortunes acquired by inheritance, and so reduce the extent to which property is concentrated in the hands of a small number of very rich people. It is interesting to recall that no appreciable death duties existed in this country before 1894. In his Budget speech of that year Sir William Harcourt defended the new policy in a passage that has become classical : " Nature gives man no power over his earthly goods beyond the term of his life. What power he possesses to prolong his will after his death — the right of a dead hand to dispose of property — is a pure creation of the law, and the State has the right to prescribe the conditions and the limitations under which that power shall be exercised." Nothing further need or can be said.

For many years after 1894 the rates of estate duty (the principal death duty) were low, and for estates of less than £100 they are still nothing. But in recent times in the upper part of the scale they have become very high indeed. In 1938 estates of £200,000 paid 25 per cent, and estates of £2,000,000 50 per cent. Now estates of £200,000 pay 34 per cent, and of £2,000,000 no less than 65 per cent. It is hardly worth while having an estate of £2,000,000 ; you can only leave a paltry £700,000 !

But death duties are not the only incident in the legal framework that affects inheritance. In this country, except where properties are entailed, a man is free to leave whatever part of his property is not absorbed by the State as he pleases ; but in a number of Continental countries there is — or was — a system of legitim, by which he is compelled to leave a certain proportion of it to his children ; in Italy more is tied up the more children he has. Anything that encourages the splitting up of estates on death among a number of heirs obviously makes against the concentration of large fortunes. On the other hand, laws or customs that lead to the eldest son getting a predominant share make in favour of it.

Of course, State policies about death duties and so on are only one part of the influences affecting the way in which ownership of capital is distributed. Moreover, changes in these policies take a long time to exercise their full influence. For the first few years after they have been introduced, their effect is bound to be very small ; for the simple reason that in these years only a small proportion of the people living when the changes were made will have died. But, once started, their effect is cumulative over successive generations. A statistical comparison for this country between 1913 and the early 1930's suggests that in the latter period the distribution of property had become somewhat less unequal ; but the difference was not great.[1] It is not possible to say how much of such difference as there was was due to death-duty policy and how much to other causes.

So far of the ownership of property. The other chief element on which the distribution of income immediately depends is the way in which personal capacities for earning income are distributed. This element, at all events in this country, is a good deal more important than the other, because income from work has for a long time been more than, or at all events not much less than, twice as large as income from property. It is evident, therefore, that, if personal qualities of a kind for which the rate of pay is high are concentrated on a small number of people, this will contribute a good deal towards concentrating a large proportion of aggregate private income in the hands of a small number of people. What, then, is there to say about this ?

[1] Cf. J. R. Hicks, *The Social Framework*, p. 186.

111

Personal capacities for earning income, as for every-thing else, are partly inborn and partly the result of education and training. Speculation about the distribu-tion of inborn qualities relevant to income-earning power is beyond my present scope. It is arguable that these qualities are highly concentrated in a small group of specially favoured families. However that may be, it is certain that those parts of income-getting capacity which are the result of education and training are highly con-centrated. The reason is, of course, that the education and training required to fit people for the better-paid occupations take a long time and are very expensive. It is practically impossible for a really poor man to invest in his son the amount of money needed to turn him into a doctor or a lawyer, or to give him a wide general educa-tion. A poor man who happens to own a potentially fertile piece of land can raise the money needed, so to speak, to educate it, because he can mortgage the land. But he cannot mortgage his son. The result is that investment in expensive education is in great part con-centrated on the comparatively small number of children whose parents are fairly well-to-do. In recent times the State and the Universities have done a good deal to alter this state of things by educational grants, scholarships and so on ; and they are proposing presently to do a good deal more. Even so, while, on the one hand, the sons of poor parents, unless they are exceptionally able, can only with difficulty secure the kind of training and educa-tion required to develop the capacities proper to well-paid occupations, on the other hand the sons of rich parents, even if they are practically morons, are given these kinds of training and education, or at all events opportunities for getting it if they choose, as a matter of course, without any difficulty whatever. There can be no doubt at all that real equality of educational opportunities, not, of course, immediately after it had been introduced, but ultimately when its full effects had worked themselves out, would go a long way towards correcting the distorted shape of current income distribution.

In the whole of this discussion I have been speaking about the distribution of private incomes, including transfer incomes, as they accrue to their owners before they have been subjected to taxation. But the thing of dominant interest to the owners of these private incomes is not what accrues to them, but what is left available to them after taxes have been imposed. Now in this country, as everybody knows, income tax, including surtax, is graduated very steeply ; so much so, that in the highest range of incomes a proportion approaching in the limit to no less than 19s. 6d. in the £ is at present taken away in taxation, so that the available income of a plutocrat of the very highest grade amounts to only one-fortieth of his accrued income. The Chancellor of the Exchequer, in his 1944 White Paper, printed a table showing for 1938 the relation between accrued income and income available after deduction of income tax and surtax at the rates ruling in that year, and also after the deduction of these taxes at the 1942–3 rates. Here it is :

Proportions of Accrued Incomes available after Deduction of Income and Surtax on the Average 1938 Incomes in the Ranges—	With Taxes at 1938 Rates	With Taxes at 1942–3 Rates
Under £250	99·8	97·8
£250–£500	97·1	93·9
£500–£1000	88·9	69·7
£1000–£2000	83·0	59·3
£2000–£10,000	71·1	47·2
Over £10,000	49·4	20·6

When these figures are combined with those set out on p. 102 the following results are obtained. The best-to-do one-tenth of 1 per cent of the population got 4 per cent of *accrued* 1938 income. But with 1938–9 tax rates they only got 2 per cent of *available* 1938 income; with the 1942 tax rates only 1 per cent. The best-to-do 1 per cent of the population got 12 per cent of 1938 *accrued* income; of *available* income between 8 per cent and 9 per cent with the 1938–9 tax rates, and 6 per cent with the 1942 rates. The best-do-do 7 per cent of the population got one-quarter of 1938 *accrued* income; but of *available* income, with the 1938–9 rates only one-fifth, with the 1942 rates only one-sixth. Plainly, then, in any ordinary sense of the word, the distribution of available income was and, in general, is much less uneven than the distribution of accrued income.

What happens to the large sums collected from the richer classes through these steeply graduated taxes? It is widely believed that a substantial part of them is used in providing social services mainly for the benefit of the poor — the under-£250 class; that the State in effect creates income (in the sense here defined) for poor persons by enforcing direct transfers to them from the better-to-do classes. Besides direct taxes there are, however, also indirect taxes yielding large sums, which are predominantly paid by the relatively poor. It is not altogether easy to strike a balance here. On the 1937 figures, the latest accessible to him when he wrote, Professor Hicks, who has studied the matter carefully, finds that the amount of taxation paid by the under-£250 class was very nearly as large as their receipts from the Government's social expenditure. From this he proceeds to argue : " It is, therefore, hardly right to describe that expenditure as a transference from the rich to the poor. What is true, however, is that the lowest income-group has been almost entirely relieved of the necessity of making a contribution to the general expenses of government ".[1]

---

[1] *The Social Framework*, p. 188. For a full discussion of these matters, published since my chapters were written, cf. Barna, *The Redistribution of Incomes through Public Finance in 1937*.

That is one way of putting things. There is, however, another way. It may be argued that, since the general expenses of Government have got to be met somehow, we ought to regard a substantial part of the taxes collected from the under-£250 class as being devoted to that purpose. If we do that, it *is* right to describe, not indeed the whole, but a sizable proportion of what is paid for social services, as a transfer from the relatively rich to the relatively poor.

In some sense, indeed, it has long been recognised that the making of such transfers is an unavoidable obligation in any civilised community. Poor persons cannot be allowed to starve or suffer extreme destitution. The English Poor Law was built on that foundation. But since the beginning of this century the scope of State action for the benefit of the poor has been expanded and elaborated. Three principal types of intervention may be distinguished. First, on certain important classes of things the main part of which is used by poor persons the State may give general subsidies. Anybody, rich or poor, who chooses to use these things, benefits from it ; but the things are so chosen that in fact it is poor people who chiefly benefit. Examples are subsidies in respect of small houses ; subsidies — in this case full-value subsidies — in respect of elementary education ; subsidies in respect of medical attendance under the Insurance Acts, of which only a part of the costs are met by insurance contributions ; subsidies in respect of insurance against unemployment ; subsidies on staple articles of food designed to prevent the ' cost of living ' from rising unduly. Secondly, gratuitous pensions may be paid by the State on the attainment of some prescribed age, either to everybody who asks for one or to everybody whose income falls below a certain level. It makes little difference whether the pensions are universal or are subject to an income limit. In either case they entail a substantial transfer of income from better-to-do people as a body to worse-to-do people. Thirdly and lastly, the State may set up a minimum standard of living conditions below which it will not allow any citizen to fall. This entails in effect making payments to very poor persons that vary inversely with the provision that these persons make for themselves. With transfers of this last kind precautions have, of course, to be taken to prevent abuses.

Until fairly recent times proposals for State action directed in one way or another to transfer purchasing power from richer to poorer people, so as to mitigate inequalities of distribution, were often met by the objection that they might damage production ; — damage it so much that, in the end, even the people to whom transfers were made would find themselves worse off than before. In particular, it was feared that saving, and so the building up of capital equipment, would be severely discouraged. At the present time much less attention is paid to this class of consideration ; partly because it is more widely recognised that to build up the strength of men, women and children by means of proper food and housing may well prove at least as productive an investment as the construction of material capital ; and partly for other reasons. This reaction against the older view is, no doubt, justified. It may, however, be carried too far. Economic advance in the past has owed a great deal to adventurous enterprise, where people have been prepared to take risks for the sake of a possible large success rather than play for safety. Special State levies from large incomes by means, for example, of a steeply graduated income tax, hits successful and unsuccessful adventurers together much more hardly than players for safety, and so discourages daring enterprise. There is a danger here that ought not to be ignored.

One further point may be made in conclusion. Just as available income is distributed differently from accrued income, so income devoted to personal consumption is distributed differently from available income. The reason is that a larger proportion of large incomes than of small incomes is devoted to investment as against consumption, and probably a larger proportion is given away. It is unlikely that a man with an available income of £4000 will spend, in satisfying the immediate needs of himself and his family, twice as much as a man with one of £2000. The part of available income devoted to consumption is thus less highly concentrated, more evenly distributed, than available income as a whole. Moreover poor people, being of necessity more careful about their buying, probably make a number of their purchases at prices below what rich people have to pay. For some things, cheap workmen's tickets, for example, there is a formal price discrimination in their favour; for others, as when they buy food in the market on Saturday nights, an informal one. It is notorious that people with ' good addresses ' find themselves charged good prices, and that some Cambridge undergraduates have to pay more for the same thing than bedmakers. The general effect of this is that consumption in terms of actual stuff is distributed less unevenly than money expenditure upon consumption. But the data are not available for estimating how important the difference is.

EPILOGUE

THIS little book has been centred round the idea of Income. In that it follows the excellent example set by Professor J. R. Hicks in his *Social Framework*. This way of introducing Economics to students beginning the subject, or to the general reader, has, as it seems to me, considerable advantages. It is less forbidding than an approach, say, by way of ' the laws of demand and supply ', and, since it lends itself to statistical illustration, is, in a sense, realistic A very substantial part of the subject matter of Economics can be indicated and discussed, of course at an elementary level, along these lines ; — and that without entering at any length upon matters of controversy. ' Advanced economic theory ' naturally tends to move on the margin of things known, and so deals largely with matters about which economists hold divergent opinions. This gives to non-economists the impression that disagreements among professional students are much more far-reaching than in fact they are. The valuable services rendered by many economists during the course of the war has, indeed, done much to soften this impression. None the less it is, I think, worth while to show, so to speak, *ambulando*, that the field over which the general body of economists are substantially agreed, so far, at all events, as qualitative analysis is concerned, is a large one. The would-be recruit, for all the noises-off that may on occasion reach him, need not really be afraid that he is entering a bear-garden.

NOTES ON LATER STATISTICS

1. Note to pp. 45-6

1953
In Millions

Imports, 2872   Exports and re-exports, 2675

Balance of current transactions including Defence Aid (net)	**225**
Increase in sterling liabilities	**222**
	447
Overseas investment (*less* borrowing)	**207**
Addition to gold and dollar reserves	**240**
	447

(Source: Balance of Payments White Paper (Cmd. 9119, Table 6).)

2. Note to p. 51.

Total personal expenditure on consumption (excluding indirect taxes
in 1953 £9352 mn.
of which:

	%
Food, drink and tobacco accounts for	47·5
Rent, rates, fuel, lighting and household goods	20·1
Clothes	10·9
Travel, including private motoring	7·0

(Source: *National Income and Expenditure*, 1946–1953, Table 21,
p. 36.)

3. Note to pp. 54-5.

Population (England and Wales) in 1951

Number of gainfully occupied persons	20,308,400
	%
increase over 1931	7·7
increase of total population since 1931	9·5
Proportion of males over 15 returned as gainfully occupied in 1951	87·9
Proportion of females over 15 returned as gainfully occupied in 1951	34·6

*Proportion of gainfully occupied persons, excluding persons out
of work, in 1951—*

		%
Manufactures of all kinds		43·9
	%	
Metals, Machinery, etc.	17·4	
Textiles	4·4	
Building and Decoration	6·2	
Clothing	3·3	
Food, Drink and Tobacco	3·3	
Others	9·4	
Agriculture, Fishing and Forestry		4·7
Mining and Quarrying		3·7
Commerce		14·1
Transport and Communication		7·7
Personal Service, including Hotels		7·2

INCOME

Public Administration	4·6
Professions	6·9
Defence	3·6
Gas, Water, Electricity	1·7
Entertainments, Sports, etc.	1·9

(Source : 1951 Census; 1 per cent Sample Tables.)

4. Note to pp. 102 and 113.

DISTRIBUTION OF PERSONAL INCOME IN U.K. IN 1953

Range of Income before Tax		Number of Incomes	Total Incomes before Tax	Income Tax and Surtax at Current Rates	Total Incomes after Tax	Proportion of Incomes retained after Tax
£		Thousands	£ million	£ million	£ million	Per cent
1953						
Exceeding	Not Exceeding					
	250	8,410	1,568	8	1,560	99·5
250	500	9,240	3,435	120	3,315	96·5
500	750	5,215	3,140	189	2,951	94·0
750	1,000	1,360	1,150	114	1,036	90·1
1,000	1,500	600	720	121	599	83·2
1,500	2,000	190	325	79	246	75·7
2,000	3,000	145	349	105	244	69·9
3,000	5,000	89	333	136	197	59·2
5,000	10,000	40	266	145	121	45·5
10,000	20,000	9	125	87	38	30·4
20,000	..	2	72	61	11	15·3
Total allocated incomes		25,300	11,483	1,165	10,318	89·9
Total personal incomes		25,300	13,584	..	..	..

(From *National Income and Expenditure*, 1954, p. 29.)

5. Note to page 103.

In Rowntree and Lavers' book on *Poverty and the Welfare State* it is estimated that the proportion of the working class population in the city of York who were living in " primary poverty, *i.e.* poverty due to lack of income, no matter how carefully the income is spent " (p. 22), fell from 31·1 per cent in 1936 to 2·77 per cent in 1950. This great improvement was in large part due to diminished unemployment, family allowances, pensions and food subsidies. York is not, of course, necessarily representative of the U.K. as a whole.

6. Note to page 110.

Since 1949 estates of £2000 and under are not subject to estate duty. The rates on estates of from £200,000 to £250,000 have been 60 per cent: on £2,000,000 and upward at 80 per cent.

(Report of the Commissioners of Inland Revenue, 1953-4, Cmd. 9030.)